Authentic Homemade
ITALIAN COOKING

JOHN PELLICANO

Introduction

When cooking you need passion, love, adventure, imagination and great taste and that's everything the Pellicano family uses when we come together and cook for that special Sunday lunch, birthday party or Christmas get-together.

I will always remember Sunday lunch during my childhood, my mother would put the sauce on the stove to start cooking at 7am and the smell would fill the house with a mouth-watering aroma that made you want pasta for breakfast. By the time it was lunch, my childhood friend Goran would come over just in time for a big bowl of Mum's specialty – *pasta shuta* – pasta in red sauce.

It was at an early age that my interest in cooking began. Watching my parents cook, they made it look so simple and easy. Dad always said that you don't need many ingredients to make a great dish. One of his favorite dishes – and mine – was spaghetti with fresh tomatoes, quickly fried with garlic and onions. So simple. We could eat that every day of the week.

Mum was always an adventurous cook, she would always prepare food for three times the amount of people that were going to eat, especially for the festive lunches. For our family of 14, she would make lasagne, croquettes, roasted vegetables, chicken and veal schnitzel, Italian meatloaf, meatballs (sometimes she would make two meatballs about 300 g (10.5 oz) each, with cheese and ham in them, one for me and the other for her first grandson Anthony), scaloppine fungi and salt and pepper squid – really, it was enough to feed 50 people.

That's mum for you. We needed to have a good variety to please everyone, she'd say, from the youngest grandson, Alexander, to my sisters and their families, and her only granddaughter, Bianca.

All the recipes in *Authentic Homemade Italian Cooking* are from our family vault of secrets handed down from our Nonna Domenica in Italy (who celebrates her 100th birthday in 2016), to my mother Maria, and then to me. Hopefully, my son Alexander can master the art of cooking Calabrese-style and continue the family tradition.

I hope you enjoy these recipes and cooking them brings as much joy to your family as it has to mine. As my father Fortunato used to say, "cucinare bene, mangiare bene" – "cook well, eat well"!

Buono appetite,
Mangia Bene,

John Pellicano

— INCIDENATAL
EXTRA RECIPE

Entrée x5
Tomato Bruschetta
Stuffed Zucchini Flowers
Whitebait Fritters
Salt and Pepper Squid
Goats Cheese, Baby Fennel and Tomato Bruschetta

LASAGNE
RISOTTO
WHITEBAI

Pasta Dough x2
Potato Gnocchi
~~Sweet Potato Gnocchi~~ — raw.

Sauces x3
~~Bolognese~~
Veal Ragout
~~Napoli Sauce with Cream~~
~~NAPOLI SAUCE~~

Pasta x7
Seafood Risotto
Lasagne
Parmigiana rigatoni
~~Home Made Pesto~~ — bowl.
~~Carbonara~~ — fett.
Meatball — spag
Chestnut Ravioli with Mushroom in Bundt Herb Butter

Mains x8
Veal Saltimbocca — sage leaf.
Chicken Parmigiana
~~Veal Schnitzel~~ Brussel Sprout Spinach.
Chicken Schnitzel) marsala.
Veal Marsala
Italian Meatloaf
~~Stuffed Tomato~~ + PEPPER.
Veal Osso Bucco

Dessert x5
Tiramisu
Lemon Gelato
Pancakes
Caramelised Figs with Chocolate Ricotta
Coffee and Nougat Semi freddo

. DRIED PASTA - FRESH
* EGGPLANT/ROLLS.   * NAPOLI SAUCE
* ARANCHINI   — CHEESES
— POT OF HERBS
— BAKE DISH TOMATOES
* STUFFED PEPPER

Contents

PASTA DOUGH

SAUCES

PASTA

MAINS

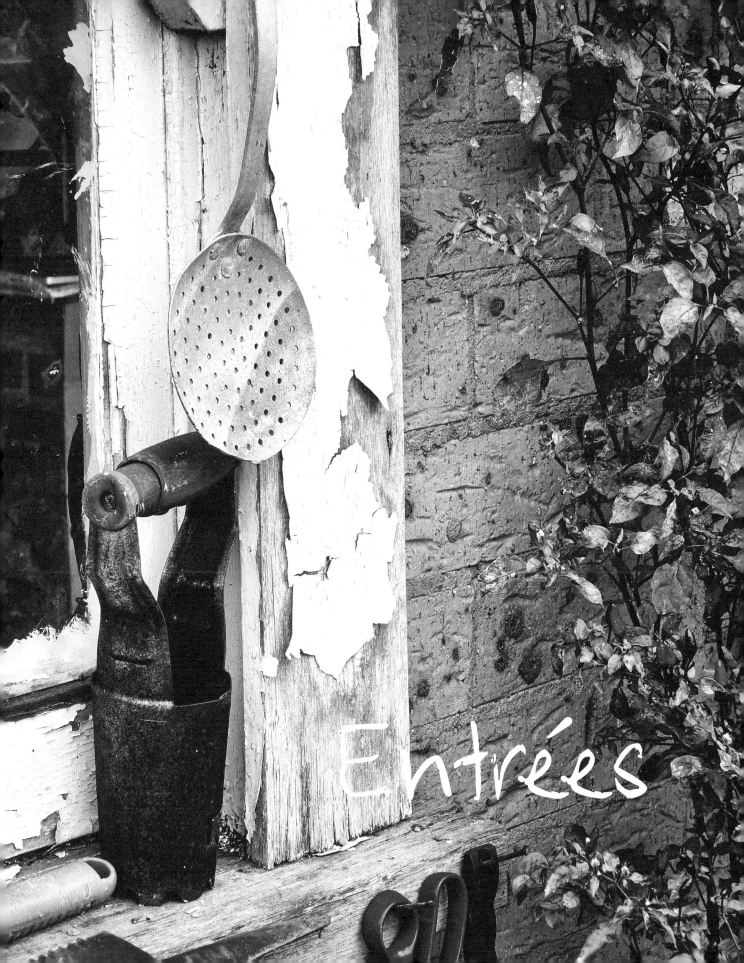

Entrées

Tomato Bruschetta

Serves 4

Ingredients:

4 Roma tomatoes, medium

¼ bunch fresh basil

1 Spanish onion, medium, peeled

Salt and pepper

60 ml (2 fl oz) olive oil

2 garlic cloves

8 slices of Pane Di Casa ★

Balsamic glaze

Method:

1. Wash the Roma tomatoes, basil and peeled onion.
2. Chop your tomatoes into parmentier. *
3. Chop the Spanish onion into brunoise. *
4. Roughly tear the fresh basil into pieces (chopping will bruise the basil).
5. Crush the garlic.
6. Combine the tomato, onion, garlic and half of the olive oil into a bowl mixing it lightly, add seasoning to taste.
7. Lightly toast your bread.
8. Place the bread on a serving plate, drizzle with the remaining olive oil.
9. Spoon the tomato mixture on to toasted bread then sprinkle your basil on top.
10. Drizzle with the balsamic glaze.
11. Serve.

★ Notes: Pane Di Casa: sliced homemade bread
Parmentier: dice 1.2 cm (0.5 in)
Brunoise: very small dice

Arancini Bolognese

Serves 14

Ingredients:

480 ml (16 fl oz) chicken stock

1 teaspoon olive oil

1 brown onion, chopped

1 clove of garlic, chopped

160 g (6 oz) arborio rice

20 g (1 oz) shredded parmesan

2 eggs

90 g (3 oz) breadcrumbs

75 g (2.5 oz) plain flour

Salt and pepper

30 ml (1 fl oz) vegetable oil

240 ml (8 fl oz) Bolognese sauce (see page 68)

Method:

1. Place your stock on the stove and bring to the boil. Cover and reduce to a gentle simmer.
2. Heat the oil in a saucepan over medium heat, add the onion and garlic. Lightly cook until the onion is soft (don't brown the onion).
3. Add the rice to the onion mix, stir until grains appear glossy. Slowly add a ladle full of your simmering stock to the rice mixture and constantly stir with a wooden spoon until the liquid has absorbed. Then continue to add the stock one ladleful at a time, until all the stock is added. Cook the rice until it is tender yet firm and the risotto is creamy.
4. Stir in the parmesan and seasoning. Set aside to cool completely (2–3 hrs).
5. When cool, mix one egg into mixture well.
6. Using moist hands roll the risotto mixture into 14 balls. Press your thumb into the center of the ball to make an indent. Place a spoon full of Bolognese sauce into the indent in the risotto ball then enclose the Bolognese sauce.
7. In three separate bowls place the breadcrumbs, flour and 1 beaten egg.
8. Roll your risotto balls into the flour, shaking off any excess, then do the same in the egg mix and finish off in the breadcrumbs, pressing to coat all the risotto balls.
9. In a shallow saucepan, add enough oil to reach 5cm (2 in) depth. Heat to medium high (when the oil is ready, test by dropping in a piece of bread – if turns golden brown in 10 seconds the oil is ready)
10. Slowly add your risotto balls to the oil turning occasionally until golden.
11. Place on a paper towel to absorb any excess oil then serve.

Arancini Mozzarella

Serves 14

Ingredients:

480 ml (16 fl oz) chicken stock

1 teaspoon olive oil

1 brown onion chopped

1 clove of garlic chopped

160 g (6 oz) arborio rice

25 g (1 oz) shredded parmesan

2 eggs

90 g (3 oz) breadcrumbs

75 g (2.5 oz) plain flour

Salt and pepper

30 ml (1 fl oz) vegetable oil

14 mozzarella pieces, 2x2cm (0.8x0.8in) dice

Method:

1. Place your stock on the stove and bring to the boil. Cover and reduce to a gentle simmer.
2. Heat the oil in a saucepan over medium heat, add the onion and garlic. Lightly cook until the onion is soft (don't brown the onion).
3. Add the rice to the onion mix, stir until grains appear glossy. Slowly add a ladle full of your simmering stock to the rice mixture and constantly stir with a wooden spoon until the liquid has absorbed. Then continue to add the stock one ladleful at a time, until all the stock is added. Cook the rice until it is tender yet firm and the risotto is creamy.
4. Stir in the parmesan and seasoning. Set aside to cool completely (2–3 hours).
5. When cool, mix one egg into mixture well.
6. Using moist hands roll the risotto mixture into 14 balls. Press your thumb into the center of the ball to make an indent. Place a piece of mozzarella into the indent in the risotto ball then enclose the cheese.
7. In three separate bowls place the breadcrumbs, flour and 1 beaten egg.
8. Roll your risotto balls into the flour, shaking off any excess, then do the same in the egg mix and finish off in the breadcrumbs, pressing to coat all the risotto balls.
9. In a shallow saucepan, add enough oil to reach 5cm (2 in) depth. Heat to medium high (when the oil is ready, test by dropping in a piece of bread – if turns golden brown in 10 seconds the oil is ready)
10. Slowly add your risotto balls to the oil turning occasionally until golden.
11. Place on a paper towel to absorb any excess oil then serve.

Potato Croquettes

Serves 4–6

Ingredients:

1 kg (35 oz) Mealy Potato ★

5 eggs

100 g (3.5 oz) parmesan cheese, grated

1 g (0.03 oz) nutmeg

Salt and pepper

1 teaspoon fresh parsley, finely chopped

450 g (16 oz) breadcrumbs

220 g (8 oz) flour

Method:

1. Steam the potatoes in their skins for about 30–40 minutes or until fully cooked (to test, slide a knife into the potato. If blade lifts out without potato lifting, potatoes are ready). Let potatoes cool completely.
2. When cool, peel the potatoes and cut into quarters. Put through a potato ricer.
3. Mix in 2 eggs, parmesan cheese, nutmeg and seasoning until you have stiff dough that forms a ball. If mixture feels to soft or wet add more parmesan cheese or a spoonful of flour.
4. Set up 3 bowls to crumb the croquettes: one to hold the breadcrumbs, one for the 3 beaten eggs and one for the flour.
5. Roll your potato mixture into 2–5cm (0.8–2 in) oval shapes.
6. Lightly pass each one in flour then egg mixture and finish in breadcrumbs. Place in the fridge for 30–45 minutes.
7. In a pan, place 5cm (2in) of oil and heat to medium to high heat. Slowly add the croquettes, turning occasionally, and cook until golden brown.
8. Place the croquettes on paper towel to absorb any excess oil.
9. Sprinkle with the chopped parsley.
10. Serve.

* Note: Mealy potatoes are russets or purple potatoes. They have thick skins and are high in starch but low in moister and sugar.

Salad Caprese

Serves 4

Ingredients:

4 ripened Roma tomatoes
250 g (8 oz) bocconcini
½ bunch basil leaves
Salt and pepper
Balsamic glaze

Method:

1. Wash the Roma tomatoes and basil.
2. Slice the tomatoes and bocconcini into 1cm (0.8in) thick slices.
3. Place the tomato around a plate and top it with the bocconcini cheese.
4. Tear the basil and sprinkle on top of the tomato and cheese.
5. Season to taste.
6. Just before serving drizzle with olive oil and balsamic glaze.
7. Serve.

Antipasto

Serves 4

Ingredients:

8 marinated artichokes

100 g (3.5 oz) kalamata olives

80 g (2.8 oz) marinated eggplant (aubergine)

80 g (2.8 oz) semi-dried tomatoes

12 slices chargrilled zucchini (courgette)

140 g (4.5 oz) chargrilled mushrooms

8 slices double smoked ham

8 slices mortadella

8 slices prosciutto

100 g (3.5 oz) bocconcini cheese

Garlic Bread

75 g (2.5 oz) softened butter

1 garlic clove, crushed

15 g (0.5 oz) fresh parsley, chopped

1 French stick

Method:

1. Preheat oven to 180°C (350°F).
2. Combine the butter, garlic and parsley in a bowl. Cut the French stick into 1.5cm (0.6in) thick slices – don't cut all the way through.
3. Spread the butter mix on both sides of the French stick slices. Wrap in foil. Place in the oven for 20 minutes.
4. Arrange all your ingredients on a large platter with all of the meat and cheese on one side and marinated vegetables on the other side.
5. Serve with your crusty garlic bread.

Stuffed Zucchini Flowers

Serves 4

Ingredients:

130 g (4.5 oz) fresh ricotta

80 g (2.8 oz) mozzarella cheese

40 g (1.5 oz) parmesan cheese, grated

20 zucchini (courgette) flowers

150 g (5 oz) corn flour

75 g (2.5 oz) self-raising (self-rising) flour, plus extra for dusting

1 tablespoon, lemon rind, grated

430 ml (14 fl oz) iced water

30 ml (1 fl oz) vegetable oil

Salt and pepper

20 g (0.7 oz) fresh parsley, chopped

20 g (0.7 oz) fresh basil, chopped

5 large green basil leaves, chopped, for garnish

5 large purple basil leaves, chopped, for garnish

Method:

1. Place into a bowl the ricotta, basil, parsley, parmesan cheese, lemon rind and mozzarella cheese, season and mix well.
2. Gently place the ricotta mix into a piping bag and slowly pipe into the zucchini flowers (trying not to overfill), twist the flower petals to enclose the mixture.
3. Mix the corn flour, self-raising flour and ice water in a bowl until it combines into a smooth batter. Allow to stand for 10 minutes.
4. Heat a large saucepan with 1cm (0.4in) of oil.
5. Dust the stuffed zucchini flowers with self-raising flour and dip into the batter mix.
6. Slowly place into the hot oil in small batches for 2–3 minutes or until puffy and golden.
7. Drain on absorbent paper.
8. Serve with the chopped basil sprinkled over the top.

Green Tomato and Radicchio Salad

Serves 4

Ingredients:

1 radicchio head
2 green tomatoes
1 fennel bulb
16 capers
30 ml (1 fl oz) olive oil
Balsamic glaze

Method:

1. Wash the radicchio and allow to dry in the fridge to become crispy.
2. Slice the tomatoes and the fennel into thin slices.
3. Heat a small frying pan over a low heat and add a little oil. When the pan is hot drop in the capers and fry lightly (capers will go a little brown), remove and place on absorbent paper take off any excess oil.
4. Arrange the radicchio leaves on the base of a plate then top with the sliced fennel and tomatoes.
5. Then drop the capers freely over the plate.
6. Drizzle with olive oil and balsamic glaze.
7. Serve.

Grilled Eggplant Rolls

Serves 4

Ingredients:

350 g (11 oz) eggplant (aubergine)

Salt and pepper

1 lemon, juiced

30 ml (1 fl oz) olive oil

50 g (2 oz) breadcrumbs

12 slices prosciutto

12 mozzarella sticks, 7x1cm (2.8x0.4in) strips

12 black olives, cut in half

12 fresh basil leaves

12 toothpicks

50 g (1.8 oz) fresh parmesan cheese

Method:

1. Slice the eggplant into 0.5cm (0.2in) thick slices. Place on a large plate, sprinkle with salt and pepper and lemon juice.
2. Heat a frying with olive oil until hot, then lightly fry the eggplant, don't overcook. Place on absorbent paper when done.
3. Place your cooked eggplant flat on a clean bench or chopping board.
4. Sprinkle the eggplant with some breadcrumbs then place on a slice of prosciutto, a mozzarella stick and 2 half olives, then roll. Place a basil leaf around the eggplant roll and skewer with toothpick to hold in place.
5. Reheat the pan with clean olive oil, fry the rolls until golden brown or until the basil leaves are brown.
6. Place on absorbent paper to get rid of excess oil.
7. Serve with grated parmesan cheese on top.

Crepe Italiano

Serves 4

Ingredients:

3 eggs
60 ml (2 fl oz) milk
80 g (2.8 oz) plain flour
40 g (1.4 oz) butter
250 g (8 oz) baby spinach
2 tablespoons olive oil
200 g (6.5 oz) fresh ricotta
75 g (2.5 oz) prosciutto, chopped
Salt and pepper
15 g (0.5 oz) parmesan, grated
Chopped dill, to garnish

Method:

1. Preheat oven to 170°C (325°F). In a bowl add 3 eggs, milk and flour and mix until it forms a runny batter mixture (if lumpy then strain).
2. Heat a nonstick frying pan with little butter and add the batter mixture to form 16–20cm (6–8in) round crepes and cook on both sides.
3. In a saucepan lightly fry the baby spinach in olive oil. Place in a strainer to allow excess liquid to drain and allow to cool.
4. Place the cooked and chopped baby spinach in a bowl with the ricotta, prosciutto and seasoning. Mix well.
5. Get the crepes and place on a clean bench or chopping board and place the ricotta mixture on half of the crepe, fold in half, then half again.
6. Place on a tray and sprinkle parmesan cheese then put in the preheated oven for 8 minutes or until the cheese is melted and golden.
7. Serve with fresh chopped dill.

Mamma's Minestrone Soup

Serves 4

Ingredients:

60 ml (2 fl oz) olive oil

4 slices pancetta, chopped

1 onion, diced

2 garlic cloves, diced

2 carrots, diced

2 celery sticks, diced

1 potato, diced

1 L (33 fl oz) chicken stock

600 g (21 oz) tomatoes, diced and deseeded

160 g (5.5 oz) small shell pasta

Parmesan, grated, to garnish

Method:

1. Heat the olive oil in a large, deep saucepan over medium heat add the pancetta, onion, garlic, carrot and celery. Mix and cook for 2–3 minutes until it softens.
2. Add the potato, stock and tomatoes then bringing to a simmer. Cook for 30 minutes or until all vegetables are tender.
3. In a separate saucepan cook the small shell pasta then drain and wash.
4. Add the cooked pasta to the sauce just before serving.
5. Serve with grated parmesan cheese.

Frittata Italiano

Serves 4

Ingredients:

2 tablespoons olive oil

4 large eggs

30 ml (1 oz) mineral water

90 g (3 oz) mozzarella, chopped

60 g (2 oz) prosciutto, sliced

60 g (2 oz) potato, diced

30 g (1 oz) parmesan cheese, grated

Salt and pepper

10 g (0.3 oz) fresh parsley, chopped

Method:

1. Preheat oven to 180°C (350°F).
2. Pour the olive oil into a saucepan that is shallow and oven proof and heat to medium heat.
3. In a bowl whisk the egg, mineral water, mozzarella , prosciutto, potato, parmesan and seasoning.
4. Add all the ingredients into the hot saucepan and place the pan in the oven.
5. Bake for 10–15 minutes.★
6. Cut into slices and serve with chopped parsley.

★ Note: To check if the frittata is cooked insert a knife into the center and it should come out clean.

Pumpkin and Goat's Cheese Salad

Serves 4

Ingredients:

200 g (7 oz) butternut pumpkin, diced

200 g (7 oz) rocket salad leaves

30 ml (1 fl oz) olive oil

160 g (5.5 oz) goat's cheese, diced

Salt and pepper

30 ml (1 fl oz) balsamic dressing

50 g (1.7 oz) slivered almonds, toasted

Balsamic glaze

Method:

1. Preheat oven to 170°C (325°F). Place lightly oiled diced pumpkin on a tray and bake for 15–20 minutes until slightly soft.★ Allow to cool.
2. Put the washed and dried rocket in a bowl and drizzle with a little olive oil, mix.
3. Add the goat's cheese and pumpkin to your rocket salad, mix well trying not to break the cheese and pumpkin.
4. Season and add the balsamic dressing.
5. Place the salad mix into a clean bowl, add the slivered almonds and drizzle with the balsamic glaze.
6. Serve

★ Note: Don't overcook the pumpkin as it will go mushy and make the salad soggy.

Whitebait Fritters

Serves 4

Ingredients:

2 eggs

80 ml (2.8 fl oz) milk

Salt and pepper

125 g (4 oz) flour

1 teaspoon baking powder

345 g (11 oz) whitebait (silverfish)

Olive oil for frying

1 lemon

Method:

1. Beat the eggs in large bowl, add the milk.
2. Season the mix, then sift the flour and baking powder in. To ensure there are no lumps slowly add the flour to egg mixture – it should form a thick and runny batter.
3. Rinse the whitebait.
4. Drain and mix the fish into batter until well combined.
5. Heat a saucepan medium to high heat and add the olive oil.
6. When the oil is hot, add a spoonful of the fish and batter and cook on both sides until golden brown.★
7. Place on absorbent paper to drain any excess oil.
8. Serve hot with lemon wedges.

★ Note: The whitebait will turn white when cooked, they are transparent when raw.

Mussel Soup

Serves 4

Ingredients:

20 black mussels

3 tablespoons olive oil

1 onion, sliced

2 large potatoes, sliced

100 ml (3 fl oz) sweet white wine

1.5 L (50 fl oz) cream

50 g (1.8 oz) butter

30 g (1 oz) fresh parsley, chopped

Method:

1. Clean and debeard the mussels and place into a bowl.
2. Put the olive oil in a large pot and heat to medium high. When the oil is hot add the onion and potato and cook until soft but not brown.
3. Add the wine and mussels to the pot and allow the mussels to steam cook until all they are open. Discard any that don't open.
4. Add the cream to the pot, reduce the heat and simmer the sauce for 20 minutes so the cream can reduce.
5. Stir through the butter and chopped parsley.
6. Serve.★

★ Note: This can be served with crusty bread.

Stuffed Mushrooms

Serves 4

Ingredients:

5 tablespoons olive oil

220 g (7 oz) white rice

480 ml (16 fl oz) chicken stock

4 large mushrooms

2 garlic cloves, chopped

1 zucchini (courgette), finely chopped

Salt and pepper

60 g (2 oz) parmesan cheese, grated

2 tablespoons fresh parsley, chopped

Method:

1. Preheat the oven to 150°C (300°F).
2. Heat the oil in a medium sized pot. Add the rice, lightly coating it with oil. Slowly add the chicken stock, 1 ladle at a time, stirring and allowing the rice to absorb some of the liquid.
3. When all the liquid has been added to rice, reduce the heat to allow the rice to cook for 10–15 minutes.
4. Take the stems off the mushrooms and chop. Place the whole mushrooms on a tray ready for filling.
5. In a separate pan heat some oil and add the garlic, chopped zucchini and mushroom stems. Lightly fry until soft then season with salt and pepper. Stir into the rice.
6. Place the rice filling on top of the mushrooms and sprinkle with parmesan cheese.
7. Place the tray of mushrooms in the oven for 15–20 minutes or until the mushrooms are soft.
8. Serve sprinkled with chopped parsley.

Salt and Pepper Squid

Serves 4

Ingredients:

500 g (16 oz) baby calamari, washed

500 g (16 oz) plain flour

500 g (16 oz) corn flour

4 tablespoons sea salt

4 tablespoons Szechwan seasoning

500 ml (16 fl oz) vegetable oil

1 lemon, cut into wedges to garnish

Method:

1. Slice the calamari tubes down one side and open them up to lie flat. Score the inside with a knife in a crosshatch pattern.★ Set aside in the fridge.
2. In a large bowl mix the plain flour, corn flour, sea salt and Szechwan seasoning.
3. Heat the oil in deep pan on high heat. Lightly coat the calamari in the flour mixture shaking off any excess.
4. Quickly fry until brown then place on absorbent paper to absorb the excess oil.
5. Serve while hot with a lemon wedge.

★ Note: To score means to make a cut, without cutting all the way through.

Seafood and Tomato Soup

Serves 4

Ingredients:

1 tablespoon olive oil

1 brown onion, chopped

1 L (33 fl oz) fish stock

400 g (13 oz) tomato puree

2 potatoes, large, cut into 2cm (0.8in) dice

250 g (8 oz) king fish (or similar)

250 g (8 oz) mussels, beards removed

Salt and pepper

250 g (8 oz) green prawns, peeled

Fresh parsley, chopped, to garnish

Method:

1. Heat the olive oil in a large saucepan, add the onion and cook for 12 minutes until soft.
2. Stir in the stock and tomato puree and diced potato. Cover and simmer for 15 minutes or until the potatoes are soft.
3. Stir in the fish and mussels and cook for 5–8 minutes or until all mussels are open, then season. Discard any mussels that don't open.
4. Add the prawns cook for a further 10–15 minutes.
5. Serve with a garnish of chopped parsley and crusty bread.

Blood Orange and Fennel Salad

Serves 4

Ingredients:

2 blood oranges

4 baby fennel bulbs, sliced very finely

100 ml (3 fl oz) extra virgin olive oil

Salt and pepper

2 tablespoons white wine vinegar

Method:

1. Peel the orange, making sure you remove all the white pith.
2. Hold the orange over a bowl to catch the juice as you cut on either side of the segments in the orange, remove the segments.
3. Place the orange segments in a separate bowl, add the fennel and lightly drizzle with olive oil and season.
4. Add the white wine vinegar to the orange juice, mix then add the fennel and orange slices.
5. Toss and serve immediately.

Antipasto Bruschetta

Serves 4

Ingredients:

1 red capsicum (bell pepper)
100 g (3.5 oz) semi-dried tomatoes
100 g (3.5 oz) chargrilled mushrooms
75 g (2.5 oz) salami, sliced
45 g (1.5 oz) kalamata olives, pitted
1 garlic clove
2 tablespoons extra virgin olive oil
8 slices crusty bread

Method:

1. Preheat the grill to high. Cut the capsicum into large flat pieces. Discard the seeds and membrane.★ Place the capsicum skin side up on a tray and grill for 10 minutes or until skin turns black. Once cooked, cover with cling wrap for 10 minutes then peel and discard skin.★

2. Roughly chop the capsicum, tomato, mushroom, salami and olives so they all are similar sizes. Place into a bowl.

3. Preheat the grill to medium high. Toast the bread on both sides.

4. While the bread is still hot, rub both sides with the pealed garlic clove.

5. Drizzle each piece with olive oil. Spoon the mixture on top.

6. Serve.

★ Notes: The capsicum membrane is the white skin between the segments.
Covering the capsicum after grilling makes it easier to peel.

Goat's Cheese, Baby Fennel and Tomato Bruschetta

Serves 4

Ingredients:

1 tablespoon olive oil

2 fresh thyme sprigs

2 garlic cloves

2 baby fennel bulbs, thinly sliced

4 slices crusty bread

120 g (4 oz) goat's cheese

45 g (1.5 oz) semi-dried tomato, sliced thickly

75 g (2.5 oz) fresh pesto (see page 67)

Method:

1. Heat the oil in a shallow pan over a medium heat. Cook the thyme sprigs and garlic for 30 seconds then add the fennel and cook for 8 minutes, or until tender and slightly caramelized. Keep warm.
2. Preheat the grill to high, toast the bread on both sides, rub the bread with the pealed garlic clove and drizzle with olive oil.
3. Spread the goat's cheese onto the toasted bread.
4. Top the bread with the semi-dried tomato, pesto and fennel mixture.
5. Serve warm.

Pasta Dough

Eggless Pasta

Serves 4

Ingredients:

480 g (15 oz) semolina
½ teaspoon salt
120 ml (4 fl oz) warm water
Extra plain flour, for rolling
Extra semolina, for sprinkling

Method:

1. In a large bowl mix the semolina and salt. Add the warm water and stir to make stiff dough. Add more water if the dough is too dry.
2. Roll the dough into a ball and place on a lightly floured surface.
3. Knead for 10–15 minutes. Cover with plastic wrap. Allow to rest for 20 minutes at room temperature.
4. Now the dough is ready to use. Cut it into 4 pieces. Cover the pieces you are not using to prevent them from drying out.
5. Use a rolling pin or pasta machine to flatten the dough. Lightly sprinkle with semolina as you roll.
6. Put through the pasta machine 3 times, each time making the sheet thinner.
7. Cut into desired shape. Allow to dry for 20 minutes before cooking.
8. Cook in boiling salted water for 3–5 minutes.
9. Drain and serve with your favorite sauce.

Semolina and Egg Pasta

Serves 4

Ingredients:

240 g (8 oz) plain flour

240 g (8 oz) semolina

½ teaspoon salt

3 large eggs

1 tablespoon olive oil

Method:

1. Sift the flour, semolina and salt onto a clean surface, make a well in the center.
2. Break the eggs into the well, add the olive oil then mix.
3. Gradually incorporate the flour from the sides of the well with your hands.
4. Begin kneading with your hands until the mixture is nice and smooth.
5. Dust the surface with semolina to keep the dough from becoming sticky.
6. Wrap the dough in plastic wrap and leave to rest for 30 minutes at room temperature.
7. Cut into 4 sections, keeping the sections you are not using covered so as not to dry out.
8. Roll out the dough with a rolling pin or pasta machine then cut into your favorite shape.

Potato Gnocchi

Serves 4

Ingredients:

2 potatoes, large
480 g (16 oz) plain flour
1 egg

Method:

1. Bring a pot of salted water to the boil. Add the potatoes (skin on) and cook until tender – about 15 minutes.
2. Drain and allow to cool.
3. Peel and then mash with a fork or potato masher.
4. Combine the potato, flour and egg in a bowl.
5. Knead until a dough forms.
6. Cut the dough into 8 pieces and roll out on floured surface into long snakes. Cut each snake into 1.3cm (0.5in) pieces.
7. Allow to rest at room temperature for 10 minutes.
8. Bring a large pot of lightly salted water to a boil. Drop in the gnocchi.
9. Cook for 3–5 minutes or until they have risen to the top of the water.
10. Drain and serve with desired sauce.

Ricotta Gnocchi

Serves 4

Ingredients:

250 g (8 oz) ricotta cheese

1½ eggs

80 g (2.8 oz) parmesan cheese, grated

Salt and pepper

250 g (8 oz) plain flour

Method:

1. Stir together the ricotta cheese, egg, parmesan, salt and pepper in a large bowl.
2. Mix in the flour to form a soft dough.
3. Divide the dough into four pieces and roll each piece into a long snake shape.
4. Cut into 1.3cm (0.5in) pieces and lightly flour so they don't stick together.
5. Place in the fridge to rest for 10 minutes.
6. Bring a large pot of lightly salted water to a boil over high heat.
7. Add the gnocchi to the boiling water, cook until they float to the surface.
8. Serve with desired sauce.

Mamma's Gnocchi

Serves 4

Ingredients:

8 potatoes

400 g (13 oz) plain flour

2 tablespoons butter

Method:

1. Bring a large pot full of salted water to the boil. Add the potatoes (skin on) and cook until tender but still firm – about 15 minutes.
2. Drain, cool slightly and then peel the potatoes.
3. Mash the potato with a fork, a masher or a ricer.
4. Place in a large bowl and make a well in the center
5. Put the butter in the well and allow to melt from the heat of the potatoes.
6. When the mashed potato has cooled, knead in the flour to create a soft dough.
7. Divide the dough into 6 portions.
8. On a floured surface, roll each portion into a long rope, then cut each rope into 1.3cm (0.5in) pieces.
9. Roll each piece with a fork for a distinctive texture.
10. Bring large pot of lightly salted water to the boil.
11. Drop the gnocchi into the water and cook for 3–5 minutes or until they float to the top.
12. Drain and serve with desired sauce.

Sweet Potato Gnocchi

Serves 4

Ingredients:

440 g (14 oz) sweet potato

1 garlic clove, chopped

½ teaspoon salt

½ teaspoon nutmeg

1 egg

440 g (14 oz) plain flour

Method:

1. Preheat the oven to 175°C (380°F).
2. Bake the sweet potatoes for 30 minutes, or until soft. Remove from the oven and allow to cool.
3. Peel the sweet potatoes and once they have cooled enough to work with, mash them with a fork, ricer or masher.
4. Place the potato into bowl and blend in the garlic, salt, nutmeg and egg.
5. Mix in the flour a little at a time until you have soft dough, cut and divide into 8 pieces.
6. On a floured surface roll out dough into long snakes and cut into 2.5cm (1in) sections.
7. Bring large pot of lightly salted water to the boil.
8. Drop the gnocchi into the boiling water allowing them to cook until they float to the surface (about 3–5 minutes).
9. Drain and serve with desired sauce.

Fresh Pasta

Serves 6

Ingredients:

950 g (21 oz) plain flour

4 eggs

Method:

1. Place the flour on a bench and make a well in center, break eggs into well, beat eggs with fork until mixed.
2. Stir the flour from the bottom of the well with a fork until the dough in the center is smooth.
3. With your hands, gradually incorporate the flour from the outside of well in towards the center.
4. Knead gently until the mass of dough comes together.
5. Knead until smooth, add more flour if it is too wet.
6. Divide into 4 pieces, wrap with plastic wrap and allow to rest for 20 minutes at room temperature.
7. Roll out one piece at a time with a rolling pin or pasta machine then cut to your desired shape.

Tomato Pasta

Serves 6

Ingredients:

950 g (21 oz) plain flour

4 eggs

2 tablespoons tomato paste

Method:

1. Place the flour on a bench and make a well in center, break eggs into well and add the tomato paste, beat eggs with fork until mixed with the tomato paste.
2. Stir the flour from the bottom of the well with a fork until the dough in the center is smooth.
3. With your hands, gradually incorporate the flour from the outside of well in towards the center.
4. Knead gently until the mass of dough comes together.
5. Knead until smooth, add more flour if it is too wet.
6. Divide into 4 pieces, wrap with plastic wrap and allow to rest for 20 minutes at room temperature.
7. Roll out one piece at a time with a rolling pin or pasta machine then cut to your desired shape.

Squid Ink Pasta

Serves 6

Ingredients:

950 g (21 oz) plain flour
4 eggs
10 drops squid ink

Method:

1. Place the flour on a bench and make a well in center, put the squid ink and break eggs into well, then mix until all the ingredients are combined.
2. Stir the flour from the bottom of the well with a fork until dough in the center is smooth.
3. With your hands, gradually incorporate flour from the outside of well in towards the center.
4. Knead gently until the mass of dough comes together.
5. Knead until smooth, add more flour if it is too wet.
6. Divide into 4 pieces, wrap with plastic wrap and allow to rest for 20 minutes at room temperature.
7. Roll out one piece at a time with a rolling pin or pasta machine then cut to your desired shape.

Spinach Pasta

Serves 6

Ingredients:

950 g (21 oz) plain flour

4 eggs

100 g (3.5 oz) baby spinach, cooked and blended

Method:

1. Place the flour on a bench and make a well in center, break eggs into well, add the spinach then beat eggs with a fork until mixed with the spinach.
2. Stir the flour from the bottom of the well with a fork until the dough in the center is smooth.
3. With your hands, gradually incorporate the flour from the outside of well in towards the center.
4. Knead gently until the mass of dough comes together.
5. Knead until smooth, add more flour if it is too wet.
6. Divide into 4 pieces, wrap with plastic wrap and allow to rest for 20 minutes at room temperature.
7. Roll out one piece at a time with a rolling pin or pasta machine then cut to your desired shape. Boil to cook and serve with the sauce of your choice.

Sauces

Napolitana Sauce

Makes 6 Servings

Ingredients:

2 kg (4.5 lb) ripe Roma tomatoes
2 tablespoons olive oil
2 large onions, diced
200 ml (7 fl oz) tomato paste
2 teaspoons dried oregano
Salt and pepper
25 g (0.9 oz) fresh basil, torn

Method:

1. Remove the core from each tomato and then cut a cross in the opposite end. Blanch each tomato in a bowl of boiling water for 30 seconds, remove with a slotted spoon and place directly into cold water. Peel off the skin. Cut each into quarters and remove all the seeds.
2. In a saucepan, fry the onions in 2 tablespoons of oil until soft and transparent. Add the tomatoes and tomato paste and bring to the boil. Lower the heat and simmer gently for 45 minutes, breaking up the tomatoes when they soften. Add the dried oregano and seasoning, then the basil. Set aside to cool down.

Pesto Sauce

Makes 6 Servings

Ingredients:

500 g (17.5 oz) fresh basil
6 garlic cloves
30 g (1 oz) pine nuts, roasted
115 g (4 oz) parmesan, grated
60 ml (2 fl oz) olive oil
Salt and pepper

Method:

1. Put the basil, garlic, pine nuts, parmesan and olive oil in the bowl of a blender. Purée until smooth.
2. Season to taste with salt and pepper.

Bolognese Sauce

Serves 8

Ingredients:

2 kg (4.5 lb) ripe Roma tomatoes

2 tablespoon olive oil

2 large onions, diced

1 kg (2.25 lb) minced (ground) veal

200 ml (7 fl oz) tomato paste

2 teaspoons dried oregano

Salt and pepper

25 g (0.9 oz) fresh basil, torn

Method:

1. Remove the core from each tomato and then cut a cross in the opposite end. Blanch each tomato in a bowl of boiling water for 30 seconds, remove with a slotted spoon and place directly into cold water. Peel off the skin. Cut each into quarters and remove all the seeds.

2. In a saucepan, fry the onions in oil until soft and transparent. Add the minced meat and fry until browned. Add the prepared tomatoes and mix in the tomato paste. Bring to the boil, lower the heat and simmer gently for 45 minutes. Once the tomatoes are soft, mix to break them up, add the oregano and seasoning.

3. Add the basil, stir to combine, then set aside to cool.

Chilli Sauce

Makes 160 g (5.5 oz)

Ingredients:

100 g (3.5 oz) mixed hot chilies
60 ml (2 fl oz) olive oil
Salt and pepper

Method:

1. Cut off the stems from all the chillies.
2. Place into a blender and blend into a rough chop, do not puree.
3. Take out of the blender, put into an airtight container and add the oil.
4. Season with salt and pepper.
5. Store in airtight container in fridge until required.

Rosetta Sauce

Makes 6 Servings

Ingredients:

2 large onions, diced

2 tablespoons olive oil

2 kg (4.5 lb) ripe tomatoes

200 ml (7 fl oz) tomato paste

240 ml (8 fl oz) cream

2 teaspoons dried oregano

Salt and pepper

25 g (0.9 oz) fresh basil, torn

Method:

1. In a saucepan, fry the onions in the olive oil until soft and transparent.
2. Add the tomatoes and tomato paste and bring to the boil.
3. Lower the heat and simmer gently for 45 minutes, breaking up the tomatoes when soft.
4. Stir through the cream.
5. Add the dried oregano and seasoning, then the basil. Now just add to your favorite pasta.

Veal Ragout Sauce

Serves 8

Ingredients:

1 tablespoon olive oil

200 g (6.5 oz) bacon rashers, lean and chopped

1 carrot, chopped

1 celery stick, chopped

1 brown onion, chopped

2 garlic cloves, chopped

1.2 kg (2.5 lb) veal rump, diced to 8cm (3in)

1 kg (35 oz) ripe tomatoes, diced

375 ml (12.5 fl oz) red wine

2 bay leaves

Salt and pepper

Method:

1. Heat the oil in large saucepan over a medium heat; add the bacon, carrot, celery, onion and garlic. Stir and cook for 5 minutes or until soft.
2. Stir in the veal rump, tomatoes, wine and bay leaves and bring to the boil.
3. Reduce the heat to a low simmer and partially cover the pan. Stir occasionally and cook for 2 hours or until the veal is tender.
4. Season, bring to boil then serve.

Cherry Tomato Sauce

Makes 6 Servings

Ingredients:

2 large onions, diced

2 tablespoons olive oil

2 kg (4.5 lb) ripe cherry tomatoes

200 ml (7 fl oz) tomato paste

2 teaspoons dried oregano

Salt and pepper

25 g (0.9 oz) fresh basil, torn

Method:

1. In a saucepan, fry the onions in the olive oil until soft and transparent.
2. Add the tomatoes and tomato paste and bring to the boil.
3. Lower the heat and simmer gently for 45 minutes, breaking up the tomatoes when soft.
4. Add the dried oregano and seasoning, then the basil. Now just add to your favorite pasta.

Fortunato Sauce

Makes 6 Servings

Ingredients:

2 large onions, diced

2 tablespoons olive oil

250 g (8.5 oz) pancetta, sliced and diced

2 kg (4.5 lb) ripe tomatoes

200 ml (7 fl oz) tomato paste

50 g (1.8 oz) black olives, pitted

Salt and pepper

50 g (1.8 oz) fresh basil, torn

Method:

1. In a saucepan, fry the onions in 2 tablespoons of olive oil until soft and transparent.
2. Add the pancetta and fry then add the tomatoes and tomato paste and bring to the boil.
3. Lower the heat and simmer gently for 45 minutes, breaking up the tomatoes when soft.
4. Add the olives and seasoning, then the basil.
5. Now just add to your favorite pasta.

Pasta

Fresh Tomato Pasta

Serves 6

Ingredients:

1 tablespoon olive oil

1 onion, diced

1 garlic clove, chopped

½ bunch fresh basil, chopped

500 g (16 oz) Roma tomatoes, ripe, diced

Salt and pepper

500 g (16 oz) spaghetti★

20 g (0.7 oz) parmesan, grated

Method:

1. Place a saucepan on medium heat, add the olive oil and onion and cook until soft and slightly golden.
2. Stir in the garlic, half of the chopped basil and diced tomatoes.
3. Season and cook for 15 minutes, stirring. Then leave to simmer for 15–20 minutes.
4. Fill a large pot with water, add salt and bring to the boil.
5. Add the pasta when the water is boiling, stir to prevent pasta from sticking together.
6. Drain once the pasta is cooked then add directly to the tomato mix, toss around to get an even coating of sauce on the pasta.
7. Serve with parmesan and the rest of the chopped basil.

★ Note: This dish is always nicest with spaghetti but you can use any type of pasta you like.

Sant' Anna

Serves 6

Ingredients:

100 ml (3 fl oz) olive oil

500 g (16 oz) Italian sausage

2 garlic cloves, crushed

200 g (7 oz) cherry tomatoes, cut into quarters

50 g (1.8 oz) olives, deseeded and cut in half

15 g (0.5 oz) chilli paste

Salt and pepper

500 g (16 oz) fresh pasta

150 g (5 oz) fresh rocket leaves

50 g (1.8 oz) parmesan, grated, to garnish

Method:

1. Preheat oven to 160°C (310°F).
2. Rub the sausages with a little oil, place on a tray in the oven and cook for 15 minutes. Cut into 2cm (0.8in) slices diagonally.
3. Heat a medium saucepan, add the oil, garlic, cherry tomatoes, olives, chilli paste and sliced sausage.
4. Cook until the tomatoes are soft.
5. Season the sauce and leave on low heat while you cook the pasta.
6. Fill a large pot with water, add a little oil and a pinch of salt then bring to the boil.
7. When boiling add the fresh pasta and cook for 5–7 minutes, then drain.
8. Turn the heat up on the tomato and sausage mix so it starts to simmer. Then toss in the pasta and rocket, mix to fully coat the pasta in the sauce.
9. Serve with grated parmesan cheese.

Parmigiana

Serves 4

Ingredients:

60 ml (2 fl oz) olive oil

1 onion, diced

1 garlic clove, sliced

350 g (11 oz) eggplant (aubergine), sliced

600 g (19.5 oz) Roma tomatoes, ripe, diced

Salt and pepper

300 g (10.5 oz) rigatoni pasta, dried

50 g (1.8 oz) parmesan cheese, grated

Method:

1. Heat a medium sized pan with a little oil, add the onion and garlic and cook until soft.
2. Add the eggplant and fry for around 5 minutes, then add the diced tomato and season.
3. Lower the heat and allow to cook for 20 minutes or until the eggplant is soft but not mushy.
4. Place a large pot of water on the heat and bring to the boil, add the pasta and cook for 10–12 minutes, or until cooked.
5. Drain the pasta when cooked and add to eggplant mix, toss to coat all the pasta in sauce.
6. Serve with grated parmesan cheese.

Pesto Gnocchi

Serves 4

Ingredients:

100 g (3.5 oz) fresh pesto (see page 67)

400 g (13 oz) fresh gnocchi (see page 51)

50 g (1.8 oz) parmesan cheese, grated

Method:

1. Fill a large pot ¾ full with water, add a pinch of salt, then bring to the boil.
2. Add the gnocchi and cook for 3–5 minutes, the gnocchi will rise to the top when cooked. Drain off the water.
3. Return the gnocchi to the pot and add the pesto★, allowing it to fully coat the gnocchi.
4. Serve with parmesan cheese.

★ Note: Pesto doesn't always need to be heated… you can add fresh pesto to hot gnocchi or pasta and the heat from the pan will warm it up.

Gianni

Serves 4

Ingredients:

2 tablespoons olive oil

1 bunch fresh asparagus, cut into 1cm (0.8in) diagonally

500 g (16 oz) double smoked ham, diced

600 ml (19 oz) cream

Salt and pepper

400 g (13 oz) fresh gnocchi (see page 51)

45 g (1.5 oz) parmesan, grated

Method:

1. Heat a medium saucepan to a high heat and add the oil, sliced asparagus and diced ham. Cook until the ham is starting to turn golden.
2. Add the cream and season, reduce the heat and leave the cream to reduce to half the quantity and thicken slightly.
3. Fill a large pot with salted water, then bring to the boil.
4. When boiling, add the gnocchi and cook for 3–5 minutes, cooking until they rise to the top of the water. Drain.
5. Add the gnocchi to the cream sauce and toss to coat the pasta evenly.
6. Serve with grated parmesan cheese.

Mamma's Special

Serves 4

Ingredients:

Olive oil

1 carrot, grated

1 zucchini (courgette), grated

80 g (2.8 oz) mushrooms, grated

600 ml (19 fl oz) cream

Salt and pepper

400 g (13 oz) penne, dried

45 g (1.5 oz) parmesan, grated

Method:

1. Heat a medium pan on high heat, add the oil, grated carrot, grated zucchini and grated mushroom.★ Cook for 8–10 minutes until all the vegetables are soft.
2. Add the cream and season. Bring to a boil, then reduce the heat to a simmer and reduce the cream to half the quantity.
3. Fill a large pot with water, add a pinch of salt and bring to the boil.
4. Add the pasta and cook for 10–12 minutes (depending on pasta type). Drain and add to the cream sauce.
5. Toss the pasta through the sauce, making sure to coat it evenly.
6. Serve with grated parmesan cheese.

★ Note: This pasta was the way mum tricked us into eating vegetables when me and my sisters were young. We couldn't tell because everything was finely grated.

Alio Olio Pepperoncino

Serves 4

Ingredients:

5 garlic cloves, chopped

30 g (1 oz) chilli paste (see page 70)

80 ml (2.7 fl oz) olive oil

Pinch of salt

400 g (13 oz) dried spaghetti

50 g (1.7 oz) parsley, chopped

50 g (1.8 oz) parmesan cheese, grated

Method:

1. Heat a medium saucepan on a medium heat, add the garlic, chilli paste and oil.* Allow to color slightly, then reduce the heat and keep warm.
2. Fill a large pot with water, add a pinch of salt and bring to the boil.
3. Add the dried spaghetti, cook for 8–10 minutes or use fresh pasta. Drain when cooked.
4. Add the chilli paste to the spaghetti, toss to coat all the pasta, then add the parsley.
5. Serve with grated parmesan cheese.

* Note: Don't put the heat on too high as garlic burns very easily.

Carbonara

Serves 4

Ingredients:

2 teaspoons olive oil

300 g (10.5 oz) bacon, lean, sliced

60 ml (2 fl oz) cream

15 g (0.5 oz) black pepper

Pinch of salt

400 g (13 oz) linguini

75 g (2.5 oz) parmesan cheese, grated

4 egg yolks (keep the half egg shells)

Method:

1. Heat the oil in a large saucepan over a medium heat, add the bacon. Cook, stirring, for 5 minutes until the bacon is crispy. Drain on absorbent paper towel.
2. In the same saucepan, add the cream and pepper and heat over a low heat to reduce the cream by half.
3. Add the bacon to the cream, simmer to keep warm.
4. Fill a large pot with water, add a pinch of salt and bring to the boil.
5. Add the pasta to the boiling water, cook for 8–10 minutes (or less time if fresh pasta). Drain.
6. Mix the pasta with bacon cream sauce and make sure it is well coated.
7. Serve with grated parmesan and the egg yolks in a half shell.
8. Pour the egg yolk over the pasta, mix quickly to give the sauce a creamier texture.★

★ Note: When mixing in the egg yolk, make sure you mix it in quickly or you will get a scrambled egg look in the finished dish.

Tre Pesce in Bianco

Serves 4

Ingredients:

2 tablespoons olive oil

100 g (3.5 oz) prawns, green and peeled

100 g (3.5 oz) baby calamari, cleaned and cut into rings

100 g (3.5 oz) Atlantic salmon, cut into cubes

2 garlic cloves, crushed

600 ml (20 fl oz) cream

Salt and pepper

400 g (13 oz) fettuccine

15 g (0.5 oz) fresh parsley, chopped

Method:

1. Heat a medium saucepan on a high heat with the oil. Add the prawns, calamari, salmon and garlic, cook for 5–7 minutes.
2. Lower the heat, add the cream and season. Leave the sauce to reduce.
3. Fill a large pot with water, add a pinch of salt and bring to the boil.
4. When boiling, add the pasta. Cook for 8–12 minutes. Drain.
5. Add the pasta to the seafood cream reduction. Toss to coat all the pasta.
6. Serve with chopped parsley.

Tre Pesce in Rosa

Serves 4

Ingredients:

2 tablespoons olive oil

100 g (3.5 oz) prawns, green and peeled

100 g (3.5 oz) baby calamari, cleaned and cut into rings

100 g (3.5 oz) Atlantic salmon, cut into cubes

2 garlic cloves, crushed

600 ml (20 fl oz) Napolitana sauce (see page 64)

Salt and pepper

400 g (13 oz) fettuccine

45 g (1.5 oz) fresh parsley, chopped

Method:

1. Heat a medium saucepan on a high heat with the oil. Add the prawns, calamari, salmon and garlic, cook for 5–7 minutes.
2. Lower the heat, add the Napolitana sauce and season. Leave to reduce.
3. Fill a large pot with water, add a pinch of salt and bring to the boil.
4. When boiling, add the pasta. Cook for 8–12 minutes. Drain.
5. Add the pasta to the seafood sauce. Toss to coat all pasta.
6. Serve with chopped parsley.

Bolognese Tortellini

Serves 4

Ingredients:

600 ml (20 fl oz) Bolognese sauce (see page 68)

400 g (13 oz) beef tortellini

60 g (2 oz) parmesan cheese, grated

Method:

1. Heat a medium saucepan to a medium heat, add the Bolognese sauce and heat.
2. Fill a large pot with water, add a pinch of salt and bring to the boil.
3. When boiling add the tortellini and cook for the instructed time, then drain.
4. Add the pasta to the sauce evenly coating it.
5. Serve with grated parmesan cheese.

Picante Napolitana Pasta

Serves 6

Ingredients:

3 fresh chillis, sliced thinly and deseeded

600 ml (20 fl oz) Napolitana sauce (see page 64)

600 g (19 oz) fresh or dried pasta

30 g (1 oz) parmesan cheese, grated

Method:

1. Preheat a medium saucepan on low heat, add the chilli and cook until soft.
2. Add the Napolitana sauce to the chilli and leave on a low heat.
3. Fill a large pot with water, add a pinch of salt and bring to the boil.
4. When boiling, add the pasta – if fresh cook for 5–7 minutes, if dried pasta check the packet for cooking instructions.
5. Drain well then add to the chilli and Napolitana sauce, coating it well.
6. Serve with parmesan cheese.

Seafood Risotto

Serves 4

Ingredients:

750 ml (25 fl oz) fish stock

375ml (12.5 fl oz) hot water

2 tablespoons olive oil

1 brown onion, chopped

350 g (11 oz) arborio rice

400 g (13 oz) black mussels, cleaned and debearded

300 g (10.5 oz) prawns

500 g (16 oz) Atlantic salmon, diced in 2x2cm (0.8x0.8in) cubes

2 blue swimmer crabs

Salt and pepper

Method:

1. Place the fish stock and water in a medium saucepan and bring to the boil, leave on a low heat at a gentle simmer.
2. In a large frying pan heat the oil over a medium heat, add the onion and cook for 2 minutes or until soft.
3. Add the rice to onion and cook until the grains are glassy, slowly add a quarter of your liquid, stirring with wooden spoon until the liquid is absorbed, continue to add the stock repeating until all the liquid is used, making sure you stir constantly.
4. Add the mussels, prawns, salmon and crabs and season with salt and pepper. Cover the pan with a lid and cook for 20–25 minutes. Make sure all the mussels are open, discard any that are not.
5. Serve immediately.

Risotto Fungi

Serves 5

Ingredients:

1 tablespoon olive oil

60 g (2 oz) butter

1 onion small, finely chopped

100 g (3.5 oz) brown mushrooms, sliced

100 g (3.5 oz) button mushroom, quartered

45 g (1.5 oz) porcini mushrooms

440 g (14 oz) arborio rice

960 ml (32 fl oz) chicken stock

30 g (1 oz) parmesan cheese, grated

Salt and pepper

Method:

1. Heat the oil and butter in a heavy based saucepan over a medium heat, add the onion and cook until soft.
2. Add the brown mushrooms, button mushrooms and porcini mushrooms and cook for 5 minutes or until soft.
3. Add rice and stir until the grains appear glassy, slowly add a quarter of the stock to rice allowing it to be absorbed. Stir with a wooden spoon. Continue adding a quarter of the stock at a time until all the liquid is added and absorbed; this should take 25 minutes to cook and the rice should be tender and creamy.
4. When finished add the parmesan and seasoning.
5. Serve.

Lasagna

Serves 6

Ingredients:

1 tablespoon olive oil
1 onion, diced
550 g (19.5 oz) lean beef mince
250 ml (8 fl oz) vegetable stock
280 g (9 oz) tomato paste
16 sheets lasagna
120 g (4 oz) mozzarella cheese, shredded

Béchamel Sauce:

40 g (1.4 oz) butter
40 g (1.4 oz) flour
400 ml (13 fl oz) milk

Method:

1. Preheat the oven to 190°C (375°F). In a non-stick frying pan add the oil and place on a medium heat, add the onion and beef mince and cook and stir for 3 minutes or until the mince browns. Slowly add the stock and tomato paste and cook for an additional 3 minutes.
2. Meanwhile, add the butter to a clean saucepan on a low heat. When melted add the flour and cook until the mixture is smooth, whisk in the milk stirring until it thickens and leave on the heat to cook out the flour taste, about 5 minutes.
3. In your baking dish place a layer of lasagna sheets at the bottom, spread a third of the mince on top of the lasagna sheets and a third of your béchamel sauce on top of that, then and add some of the mozzarella.
4. Repeat this layering twice more.
5. Cover the baking dish with greaseproof paper or foil and bake for 20 minutes.
6. Remove the foil and cook for a further 10 minutes or until the pasta is soft.
7. When cooked allow to rest for 10 minutes.★
8. Cut and serve.

★ Note: Allowing it to rest after baking makes it easier to cut.

Pasta Al Forno

Serves 4

Ingredients:

400 g (13 oz) penne pasta

300 g (10.5 oz) Bolognese sauce (see page 68)

150 g (5 oz) mozzarella cheese, shredded

100 g (3.5 oz) frozen peas

Method:

1. Preheat oven to 200°C (400°F).
2. Fill a large pot with water and bring to the boil.
3. When boiling, add the pasta and cook for 8 minutes.*
4. Drain all of the water from the pasta.
5. Place the pasta, Bolognese sauce, mozzarella and peas in a baking dish, mixing all the ingredients together.
6. Cover and place in the oven for 20 minutes.
7. Remove the cover and cook for a further 10 minutes.
8. Serve.

* Note: Don't over cook the pasta when boiling as when you cook it in the oven it will fall apart.

Picante Al Tonno

Serves 4

Ingredients:

75 ml (2.5 fl oz) olive oil

1 garlic clove, chopped

2 fresh chillis, chopped and deseeded

250 g (8 oz) tuna

Salt and pepper

400 g (13 oz) penne pasta

15 g (0.5 oz) fresh parsley, chopped

Method:

1. Heat a frying pan to a medium heat and add the olive oil, garlic, chilli and tuna. Cook for 3 minutes and then turn down to a low heat.
2. Fill a large pot with water, add a pinch of salt and bring to the boil.
3. When boiling, add the pasta and cook for 10 minutes then drain.
4. Add the pasta to the tuna sauce, toss and add the seasoning and parsley.
5. Serve.

Meatball Pasta

Serves 6

Ingredients:

2 slices of white bread, crust off, cubed

15 ml (0.5 fl oz) milk

1 brown onion, grated

500 g (16 oz) beef mince

1 egg, lightly beaten

80 g (2.8 oz) parmesan cheese, grated

80 g (2.8 oz) fresh parsley, chopped

Salt and pepper

2 tablespoons olive oil

500 ml (16 fl oz) Napolitana sauce (see page 64)

500 g (16 oz) fresh spaghetti

Method:

1. Place the bread in a large bowl, add the milk and let it stand for 5 minutes. Mix in the onion, mince, egg, half of the cheese, half of the parsley and season. Mix to combine it well.
2. Allow the mixture to rest for 10 minutes.
3. Roll into 5cm (2in) round balls and place on a plate ready for cooking.
4. Heat the oil in a large pan over a medium heat, slowly add the meatballs turning for 5–7 minutes until brown on the outside.
5. When the meatballs are cooked add the Napolitana sauce and leave to simmer on a low heat for 15 minutes.
6. Fill a large pot with water, add a pinch of salt and bring to the boil.
7. When boiling, add the fresh pasta and cook for 5–7 minutes, drain.
8. Place the spaghetti on a plate and top with 3 or 4 meatballs and some sauce.
9. Serve with parmesan cheese and chopped parsley.

Ravioli with Herb Butter

Serves 4

Ingredients:

25 ml (0.8 fl oz) olive oil

50 g (1.8 oz) leeks, chopped

30 g (1 oz) carrot, grated

15 g (0.5 oz) celery, chopped

200 g (6.5 oz) porcini mushrooms, sliced

400 g (13 oz) lean pork mince

50 ml (1.8 fl oz) white wine

15 g (0.5 oz) shallots, chopped

Salt and pepper

500 g (16 oz) fresh pasta dough (see page 57)

2 egg whites

175 g (5.5 oz) butter

5 g (0.2 oz) mixed herbs

30 g (1 oz) parmesan cheese, grated

Method:

1. In a medium saucepan heat the oil and add the leeks, carrots, celery and mushrooms and cook for 5 minutes.
2. Now add the mince and cook for 20 minutes. Make sure it isn't too dry then add the wine, shallots and seasoning and leave on a low heat to reduce.
3. Cut the fresh pasta into 8 even oblong pieces and roll 2 pieces at a time. Keep the remaining dough covered to avoid drying out.
4. Roll the pasta into a length of 35cm x 8cm (14in x 3 in), separate the two pieces.
5. On one sheet of the pasta place 2 teaspoons of the mince mixture at even intervals along the pasta. Brush the pasta lightly with egg white then place the other sheet of pasta on top, gently pressing the edges together to seal. Cut into individual squares.
6. Repeat this process with the remaining pasta and mixture.
7. In a medium frying pan add the butter and place over a medium heat. When melted add the mixed herbs. Reduce and leave to simmer.
8. Fill a large pot with water, add a pinch of salt and bring to the boil.
9. When boiling add the pasta and cook for 6–7 minutes or until the squares float to the surface. Drain.
10. Place the pasta on a plate, drizzle the herb butter sauce over the top and sprinkle with parmesan cheese.

Vegetarian Lasagna

Serves 6

Ingredients:

2 eggplants (aubergines), thinly sliced crossways

4 zucchini (courgettes), thinly sliced lengthways

3 red capsicums (bell peppers), cut into quarters

16 lasagna sheets

125 g (4 oz) mozzarella cheese

500 g (16 fl oz) Napolitana sauce (see page 64)

45 g (1.5 oz) parmesan cheese, grated

Béchamel sauce

20 g (0.7 oz) butter

20 g (0.7 oz) flour

200 ml (16 fl oz) milk

Method:

1. Preheat the oven to 190°C (375°F).
2. Meanwhile, add the butter to a saucepan on a low heat, when melted add the flour and cook until the mixture is smooth, whisk in the milk stirring until it thickens. Leave on the heat for 5 minutes to cook out the flour taste.
3. In a baking dish place 4 sheets of lasagna, then add a quarter of the Napolitana sauce and a quarter of the béchamel sauce, then add the sliced eggplant and a quarter of the mozzarella.
4. Place 4 lasagna sheets on top of the eggplant, add another quarter of Napolitana sauce and béchamel sauce and then place the capsicum slices. Add another quarter of the mozzarella.
5. Repeat the process with the pasta sheets and sauces, then place the zucchini and more mozzarella.
6. Add the final layer of pasta, sauces and mozzarella cheese then top with the parmesan cheese.
7. Cover the baking dish with greaseproof paper then foil.
8. Cook for 20 minutes.
9. Remove the foil and cook for a further 10 minutes or until the pasta is soft.
10. When cooked allow to rest for 10 minutes.
11. Cut and serve.

Spinach and Ricotta Cannelloni

Serves 4

Ingredients:

750 g (24 oz) fresh ricotta

150 g (5 oz) baby spinach

8 fresh lasagna sheets (see page 57)

480 ml (16 fl oz) Napolitana sauce (see page 64)

75 g (2.5 oz) mozzarella

45 g (1.5 oz) parmesan cheese

Method:

1. Preheat oven to 180°C (350°F).
2. Place the ricotta and spinach into a bowl. Mix to combine
3. Place the lasagna sheets on a bench, split the ricotta mixture between 8 sheets, placing it in the center. Roll to enclose the filling.
4. Spread half of the Napolitana sauce on the base of an ovenproof tray. Arrange the pasta tubes seam side down in the tray.
5. Place the remaining Napolitana sauce over the pasta and top with mozzarella cheese and parmesan.
6. Cover with greaseproof paper and foil. Bake for 30 minutes.
7. Remove the cover for the last 10 minutes of cooking.
8. When removed from the oven, allow to stand for 5 minutes before serving.

Meat Cannelloni

Serves 4

Ingredients:

1 tablespoon olive oil

1 onion, finely chopped

2 garlic cloves, crushed

500 g (16 oz) beef mince

600 ml (19 fl oz) Napolitana sauce (see page 64)

8 fresh lasagna sheets (see page 57)

Cheese Sauce

60 g (2 oz) butter

60 g (2 oz) plain flour

600 ml (19 fl oz) milk

45 g (1.5 oz) parmesan, finely grated

60 g (2 oz) cheddar cheese

Salt and pepper

Method:

1. Preheat oven to 180°C (350°F).
2. Heat the oil in a large saucepan over a high heat, add the onion and garlic, cook for 5 minutes or until soft.
3. Add the mince, stirring with a wooden spoon to break up any lumps, and cook until the meat starts to brown. Add two thirds of the Napolitana sauce. Season. Stir to combine. Reduce heat to a low simmer leaving to cook for 15 minutes.
4. To make the cheese sauce melt the butter in a large saucepan over a medium heat, add the flour and cook until the mixture scrapes off the edge of saucepan and is smooth. Slowly add the milk, mixing with whisk until it thickens – around 5 minutes. Remove from the heat and add the parmesan and half the cheddar cheese. Stir until it melts. Season.
5. Place your 8 fresh pasta sheets on a bench, evenly distribute your meat into the center of each sheet then roll to enclose the filling.
6. Spread the other third of Napolitana sauce on the bottom of a tray. Arrange the pasta tubes in the tray seam side down.
7. Now cover your pasta with the cheese sauce.
8. Cover with greaseproof and foil and bake for 30 minutes, remove the cover for the final 10 minutes.
9. When cooked, remove from oven and allow to stand for 10 minutes before serving.

Four Cheese Gnocchi

Serves 4

Ingredients:

400 ml (13 fl oz) cream

125 g (4 oz) butter

60 g (2 oz) parmesan cheese, grated

60 g (2 oz) mozzarella cheese, shredded

60 g (2 oz) provolone cheese, grated

60 g (2 oz) blue vein cheese, crumbled

500 g (16 oz) gnocchi (see page 51)

Method:

1. In a medium saucepan, combine the cream and butter. Bring to a simmer over a medium heat, stir until the butter melts.
2. Slowly add the parmesan, mozzarella, provolone and blue vein cheese, reduce the heat and continue to stir until all the cheeses have melted.
3. Fill a large pot with water and add a pinch of salt. Bring to the boil.
4. When boiling, add the gnocchi. Cook for 3–5 minutes or until the gnocchi float to the top. Remove from the heat and drain.
5. Mix the gnocchi into your cream cheese sauce, completely coating them.
6. Serve with more parmesan cheese.

Mains

Veal Saltimbocca

Serves 4

Ingredients:

30 ml (1 oz) olive oil

600 g (21 oz) veal, sliced into 4 pieces

Salt and pepper

4 prosciutto slices

50 g (1.7 oz) plain flour

240 ml (8 fl oz) white wine

30 g (1 oz) butter

1 tablespoon parsley, chopped

Method:

1. Heat the oil in a large pan, over a medium heat.
2. Lightly season the veal, and then wrap prosciutto around it. Lightly beat with a meat cleaver to keep prosciutto attached to the veal.
3. Dip the veal into flour, and then add to the hot oil. Cook for 2–3 minutes on each side, slightly coloring. Remove when cooked.
4. Add wine to pan, simmer over a high heat and reduce by half. Add the butter and parsley.
5. Return the veal to the pan, reduce the heat and simmer for 5 minutes.
6. Serve.

Chicken Saltimbocca

Serves 4

Ingredients:

30 ml (1 oz) olive oil

600 g (21 oz) chicken breast, 4 pieces

Salt and pepper

4 prosciutto slices

50 g (1.7 oz) plain flour

240 ml (8 fl oz) white wine

30 g (1 oz) butter

1 tablespoon parsley, chopped

Method:

1. Heat the oil in a large pan, over a medium heat.
2. Lightly season the chicken, and then wrap prosciutto around it. Lightly beat with a meat cleaver to keep prosciutto attached to the chicken.
3. Dip the chicken into flour, and then add to the hot oil. Cook for 2–3 minutes on each side, slightly coloring. Remove when cooked.
4. Add wine to pan, simmer over a high heat and reduce by half. Add the butter and parsley.
5. Return the chicken to the pan, reduce the heat and simmer for 5 minutes.
6. Serve.

Veal Parmigiana

Serves 4

Ingredients:

2 teaspoons olive oil

1 eggplant (aubergine), sliced lengthways

500 g (16 oz) veal escalopes★, 4 x 125 g (4.4 oz)

400 ml (13 fl oz) Napolitana sauce (see page 64)

80 g (2.8 oz) mozzarella cheese, 4 slices

Method:

1. Heat the oil in a saucepan over a medium heat, lightly cook the eggplant slices on both sides. Remove when cooked, place on absorbent paper towel.
2. In the saucepan, cook your veal until a light golden brown color.
3. Preheat oven to 170°C (325°F).
4. Place the cooked veal on a tray; place the eggplant on top then evenly spread Napolitana sauce on top. Finish with the mozzarella cheese slices.
5. Place into the oven for 10 minutes or until the cheese has melted.
6. Serve.

★ Note: You can use veal schnitzel as well.

Chicken Parmigiana

Serves 4

Ingredients:

2 teaspoons olive oil

1 eggplant (aubergine), sliced lengthways

500 g (16 oz) chicken escalopes★, 4 x 125 g (4.4 oz)

400 ml (13 fl oz) Napolitana sauce (see page 64)

80 g (2.8 oz) mozzarella cheese, 4 slices

Method:

1. Heat the oil in a saucepan over a medium heat, lightly cook the eggplant slices on both sides. Remove when cooked, place on absorbent paper towel.
2. In the saucepan, cook your chicken until a light golden brown color.
3. Preheat oven to 170°C (325°F).
4. Place the cooked chicken on a tray; place the eggplant on top then evenly spread Napolitana sauce on top. Finish with the mozzarella cheese slices.
5. Place into the oven for 10 minutes or until the cheese has melted.
6. Serve.

★ Note: You can use chicken schnitzel as well.

Goat Stew

Serves 4

Ingredients:

2 tablespoons olive oil

800 g (28 oz) goat meat, on the bone, cut into pieces

60 g (2 oz) plain flour

1 onion, chopped

2 carrots, 2cm (0.8in) dice

1 red capsicum (bell pepper), 2cm (0.8in) dice

2 potatoes, 2cm (0.8in) dice

4 garlic cloves, crushed

400 ml (13 fl oz) Napolitana sauce (see page 64)

240 ml (8 fl oz) beef stock

Method:

1. Heat the oil in a large saucepan over a medium heat, lightly coat the goat meat in flour, place into the saucepan and brown the meat.
2. Set aside the goat meat, then cook the onion, carrots, capsicum, potatoes and garlic for 10 minutes on medium heat.
3. Pour the Napolitana sauce and stock over the vegetables and bring to the boil, then reduce the heat to a simmer.
4. Return the goat meat to the sauce and leave to simmer for 30–40 minutes until the meat and vegetables are tender.
5. Allow to stand for 10 minutes.
6. Serve.

Slow Cooked Rabbit Stew

Serves 4

Ingredients:

1 tablespoon olive oil

1 rabbit, cut into pieces

60 g (2 oz) plain flour

60 g (2 oz) bacon, cut into strips

2 celery sticks, 2cm (0.8in) dice

2 potatoes, 2cm (0.8in) dice

2 carrots, 2cm (0.8in) dice

1 garlic clove, crushed

1 onion, sliced

150 ml (5 fl oz) red wine

240 ml (8 fl oz) chicken stock

5 g (0.2 oz) thyme sprigs

1 bay leaf

45 g (1.5 oz) chopped parsley

Method:

1. Preheat oven to 150°C (300°F).
2. Heat the oil in large heat proof dish over a medium heat, place the rabbit in flour and coat it lightly.
3. Put the rabbit into the oil and brown, do this in small batches. Set the rabbit aside when cooked.
4. Add the bacon, celery, potatoes, carrot, garlic and onion and cook until they have started to color.
5. Pour red wine and stock onto the vegetables then put the thyme, bay leaf and rabbit into the pot and stir.
6. Cover the dish, put it in the oven and cook for 2 hours or until the rabbit is tender.
7. Serve with chopped parsley.

Stuffed Eggplant

Makes 4

Ingredients:

2 eggplants (aubergines)

2 tablespoon olive oil

1 onion, chopped

1 garlic clove, crushed

1 red capsicum (bell pepper), 1cm (0.4in) dice

1 celery stick, 1cm (0.4in) dice

200 g (6.5 oz) cooked rice

100 ml (3 fl oz) Napolitana sauce (see page 64)

2 tablespoons fresh parsley, chopped

2 tablespoons fresh basil, chopped

150 g (5 oz) mozzarella cheese, grated

30 g (1 oz) parmesan cheese, grated

Method:

1. Preheat oven to 180°C (350°F).
2. Cut the eggplant in half lengthways. Scoop out the flesh to within a centimeter (0.4in) of skin to create a shell. Chop the flesh.
3. Heat the oil in large frying pan on medium heat. Then add the onion, garlic, capsicum and celery, cook for 4 minutes and then add chopped eggplant and cook for a further 3 minutes.
4. Stir in the cooked rice and Napolitana sauce then add the chopped parsley and basil, stir occasionally.
5. Assemble the eggplant halves on a lightly greased baking tray and divide the vegetable mixture between the halves.
6. Top each eggplant with a combination of mozzarella and parmesan cheese.
7. Bake in a preheated oven for 35–40 minutes or until the eggplant is tender and cheese is golden brown.
8. Serve.

Stuffed Capsicum

Makes 4

Ingredients:

2 capsicums (bell peppers)

2 tablespoon olive oil

1 onion, chopped

1 garlic clove, crushed

1 celery stick, 1cm (0.4in) dice

200 g (6.5 oz) cooked rice

100 ml (3 fl oz) Napolitana sauce (see page 64)

2 tablespoons fresh parsley, chopped

2 tablespoons fresh basil, chopped

150 g (5 oz) mozzarella cheese, grated

30 g (1 oz) parmesan cheese, grated

Method:

1. Preheat oven to 180°C (350°F).
2. Cut the capsicum in half lengthways. Scoop out the flesh and seeds to create a shell.
3. Heat the oil in large frying pan on medium heat. Then add the onion, garlic and celery, cook for 4 minutes.
4. Stir in the cooked rice and Napolitana sauce then add the chopped parsley and basil, stir occasionally.
5. Assemble the capsicum halves on a lightly greased baking tray and divide the vegetable mixture between the halves.
6. Top each capsicum with a combination of mozzarella and parmesan cheese.
7. Bake in a preheated oven for 35–40 minutes or until the capsicum is tender and cheese is golden brown.
8. Serve.

Veal Schnitzel

Serves 4

Ingredients:

60 g (2 oz) plain flour

1 egg

30 ml (1 fl oz) milk

100 g (3.5 oz) panko breadcrumbs

30 g (1 oz) parsley, chopped

800 g (28 oz) veal escalopes, 8 x 100 g (3.5 oz)

Salt and pepper

60 ml (2 fl oz) vegetable oil

1 lemon, cut into wedges

Method

1. Place the flour on a large plate. In a bowl combine the egg and milk and whisk together. In another bowl place the breadcrumbs and half of the chopped parsley.

2. Season the veal then coat in flour, shaking off any excess. Then dip one piece into the egg mix, and then finish in the breadcrumbs pressing firmly to coat. Place the veal piece on a plate and repeat with the remaining pieces.

3. Heat a nonstick frying pan over medium heat, put the oil into the pan and add one veal piece to cook for 4 minutes or golden brown. Turn over and cook on the other side. Transfer to a plate lined with absorbent paper towel. Repeat this with the other veal pieces, reheating the pan between batches.

4. Serve with lemon wedges and chopped parsley.

Chicken Schnitzel

Serves 4

Ingredients:

60 g (2 oz) plain flour
1 egg
30 ml (1 fl oz) milk
100 g (3.5 oz) panko breadcrumbs
30 g (1 oz) parsley, chopped
800 g (28 oz) chicken escalopes, 8 x 100 g (3.5 oz)
Salt and pepper
60 ml (2 fl oz) vegetable oil
1 lemon, cut into wedges

Method

1. Place the flour on a large plate. In a bowl combine the egg and milk and whisk together. In another bowl place the breadcrumbs and half of the chopped parsley.
2. Season the chicken then coat in flour, shaking off any excess. Then dip one piece into the egg mix, and then finish in the breadcrumbs pressing firmly to coat. Place the chicken piece on a plate and repeat with the remaining pieces.
3. Heat a nonstick frying pan over medium heat, put the oil into the pan and add one chicken piece to cook for 4 minutes or golden brown. Turn over and cook on the other side. Transfer to a plate lined with absorbent paper towel. Repeat this with the other chicken pieces, reheating the pan between batches.
4. Serve with lemon wedges and chopped parsley.

Chicken Marsala

Serves 4

Ingredients:

60 g (2 oz) plain flour

Pinch of salt and pepper

½ teaspoon oregano

1 kg (35 oz) chicken escalopes, 8 x 125 g (4.5 oz) slices

4 teaspoon butter

4 teaspoons olive oil

250 g (8 oz) mushrooms, sliced

120 ml (4 fl oz) marsala wine

120 ml (4 fl oz) sherry

Method

1. In a shallow bowl mix the flour, salt, pepper and oregano.
2. Coat the chicken pieces in the flour.
3. In a large frying pan melt the butter and oil over a medium heat. Place the chicken into the pan and lightly brown, turning chicken pieces to cook both sides.
4. Add the mushrooms, marsala and sherry. Simmer for 10 minutes turning the chicken occasionally.
5. When the marsala and sherry have reduced, turn the heat off.
6. Serve.

Veal Marsala

Serves 4

Ingredients:

60 g (2 oz) plain flour

Pinch of salt and pepper

½ teaspoon oregano

1 kg (35 oz) veal escalopes, 8 x 125 g (4.5 oz) slices

4 teaspoon butter

4 teaspoons olive oil

250 g (8 oz) mushrooms, sliced

120 ml (4 fl oz) marsala wine

120 ml (4 fl oz) sherry

Method

1. In a shallow bowl mix the flour, salt, pepper and oregano.
2. Coat the veal pieces in the flour.
3. In a large frying pan melt the butter and oil over a medium heat. Place the veal into the pan and lightly brown, turning veal pieces to cook both sides.
4. Add the mushrooms, marsala and sherry. Simmer for 10 minutes turning the veal occasionally.
5. When the marsala and sherry have reduced, turn the heat off.
6. Serve.

Italian Meatloaf

Serves 4

Ingredients:

115 g (4 oz) sundried tomatoes

800 g (28 oz) beef mince

200 g (6.5 oz) breadcrumbs

100 g (3.5 oz) onion, finely chopped

90 g (3 oz) fresh basil, chopped

120 ml (4 oz) tomato sauce

2 egg whites

2 garlic cloves, chopped

Salt and pepper

10 slices provolone cheese

10 slices pancetta

2 boiled eggs

Method

1. Preheat the oven to 175°C (330°F). Prepare a loaf pan by rubbing with it with oil, this will prevent the meatloaf from sticking.
2. Mix the sundried tomatoes, beef, breadcrumbs, onion, basil, tomato sauce, egg whites, garlic and seasoning all together in a bowl, combine all ingredients well.
3. When mixed, flatten out the mince on a bench and lay the sliced provolone and pancetta on top then the two boiled eggs. Roll the mince to enclose and place into your greased pan.
4. Bake in the oven for 1 hour or until no longer pink in center. To see if it is cooked in the center put a skewer in and then pull it out – if clear juice comes out it is ready, if red juice runs out then return the tin to the oven for 30 minutes.
5. Remove from the loaf tin and allow to rest for 10 minutes before slicing.
6. Slice and serve.

Veal Involtini

Serves 4

Ingredients:

1 kg (35 oz) veal escalopes, 8 x 125 g (4.5 oz) slices

16 fresh basil leaves

150 g (5 oz) buffalo mozzarella, sliced into 16 pieces

1 tablespoon olive oil

Salt and pepper

60 g (2 oz) plain flour

1 brown onion, finely chopped

2 garlic cloves, crushed

500 ml (16 fl oz) Napolitana sauce (see page 64)

80 ml (2.7 fl oz) chicken stock

Method:

1. Top each piece of veal with 2 basil leaves and 2 pieces of mozzarella, roll up to enclose the filling. Secure with a toothpick.
2. Heat the oil in a nonstick frying pan over a medium heat. Lightly coat the veal with seasoned flour, and then cook in batches for 2 minutes on each side until brown all over. Transfer onto a plate and cover to keep warm.
3. In same pan, add the onion and garlic and cook for 5 minutes until soft.
4. Add the Napolitana sauce and chicken stock. Bring to boil, then reduce the heat.
5. Return the veal to the sauce, cook for 10 minutes on low heat, turning occasionally.
6. Serve with sauce poured over the veal.

Chicken Involtini

Serves 4

Ingredients:

1 kg (35 oz) chicken escalopes, 8 x 125 g (4.5 oz) slices

16 fresh basil leaves

150 g (5 oz) provolone sliced into 16 pieces

150 g (5 oz) pancetta

1 tablespoon olive oil

Salt and pepper

60 g (2 oz) plain flour

1 brown onion, finely chopped

2 garlic cloves, crushed

500 ml (16 fl oz) Napolitana sauce (see page 64)

80 ml (2.7 fl oz) chicken stock

Method:

1. Top each piece of chicken with 2 basil leaves, 2 pieces of provolone and 1 piece of pancetta then roll up to enclose the filling. Secure with a toothpick.
2. Heat oil in a nonstick frying pan over a medium heat. Lightly coat the chicken with seasoned flour, then cook in batches for 2 minutes on each side until brown all over. Transfer to a plate and cover to keep warm.
3. In the same pan, add the onion and garlic and cook for 5 minutes until soft.
4. Add the Napolitana sauce and chicken stock. Bring to boil then reduce the heat.
5. Return the chicken to the sauce, cook for 10 minutes on a low heat, turning occasionally.
6. Serve with the sauce poured over the chicken.

Stuffed Tomatoes

Makes 4

Ingredients:

4 tomatoes, large
4 teaspoons olive oil
100 g (3.5 oz) Arborio rice
3 spring onions (scallions), chopped
1 zucchini (courgette), chopped
500 ml (16 fl oz) vegetable stock
1 teaspoon Italian herbs, dried
4 basil leaves, fresh

Method:

1. Preheat the oven to 170°C (325°F).
2. Slice the top off the tomatoes and set aside, scoop out the seeds and pulp from the tomatoes with a teaspoon, being careful not to break through the base. Chop the pulp and keep the seeds, but discard the hard cores.
3. Heat the oil in a medium saucepan and add the rice, fry gently over a low heat for 2 minutes stirring to prevent the rice from browning, then add the spring onions and zucchini and fry gently for 2 more minutes.
4. Add the stock, herbs and tomato pulp and seeds and cook on a low heat for 20 minutes, stirring frequently until the rice is tender and all the stock has been absorbed.
5. Season and stir.
6. Place the tomatoes in an ovenproof dish and fill each one with risotto and top with a basil leaf.
7. Place the tomato tops in place and bake uncovered for 15–20 minutes or until the tomatoes are tender.
8. Remove from the oven and serve.

Veal Osso Bucco

Serves 4

Ingredients:

1 kg (35 oz) veal osso bucco

100 g (4 oz) flour

Salt and pepper

60 ml (2 fl oz) olive oil

1 onion, diced into 2cm (0.8in) cubes

1 carrot, diced into 2cm (0.8in) cubes

1 celery stick, diced into 2cm (0.8in) cubes

2 garlic cloves, chopped

1 teaspoon dried mixed herbs

60 ml (2 fl oz) white wine

400 ml (13 fl oz) Napolitana sauce (see page 64)

240 ml (8 fl oz) beef stock

Method:

1. Lightly coat the veal in seasoned flour.
2. Heat the oil in a large saucepan, add the veal and cook for 3–5 minutes until evenly browned, remove and set aside.
3. In the same saucepan, add the onion, carrot and celery and cook for 5 minutes, add the garlic and herbs and cook for 1 more minute.
4. Stir in the wine, Napolitana sauce and stock, return the veal to the pan and bring to the boil. Reduce the heat and simmer for 1.5 hours, stirring occasionally.
5. When cooked the meat will come off the bone.
6. Serve.

Lamb Shanks

Serves 4

Ingredients:

4 lamb shanks, frenched

1 teaspoon flour

Salt and pepper

60 ml (2 fl oz) olive oil

2 onions, diced into 2cm (0.8in) cubes

3 carrots, diced into 2cm (0.8in) cubes

2 celery sticks, diced into 2cm (0.8in) cubes

480 ml (16 fl oz) Napolitana sauce

60 ml (2 fl oz) red wine

Chopped parsley for garnish

Method:

1. Preheat the oven to 160°C (315°F).
2. Lightly coat the shanks in seasoned flour.
3. Heat the olive oil in a frying pan, add the shank and cook until browned well on all sides.
4. In a large ovenproof dish place the onion, carrots and celery then put the shanks on top.
5. Pour the Napolitana sauce over the shanks and then add the red wine.
6. Cover with greaseproof paper and foil, then place in the oven for 3 hours.
7. Remove from the oven to see if cooked, when ready the meat will come off the bone.
8. Serve with chopped parsley.

Chicken Cacciatore

Serves 4

Ingredients:

2 tablespoons olive oil

1.4 kg (50 oz) chicken thighs, about 8 pieces

200 g (6.5 oz) mushrooms

1 onion, finely chopped

4 slices pancetta, chopped

2 garlic cloves, chopped

120 ml (4 fl oz) white wine

500 ml (16fl oz) Napolitana sauce (see page 64)

225 g (8 oz) Kalamata olives

Method:

1. Heat 1 tablespoon of oil in a large deep frying pan; add half the chicken and cook, turning occasionally for 5 minutes until golden brown, transfer to a plate. Repeat with the remaining chicken.
2. Add the rest of the oil to a pan over a medium heat, add the mushrooms and cook then remove. Add the onion, pancetta and garlic to the pan, stir and cook for 5 minutes.
3. Add the chicken and mushrooms back into the pan then add wine and bring to the boil, add the Napolitana sauce and stir.
4. Reduce the heat to medium low and cook, covered, stirring occasionally for 20 minutes.
5. Add the olives and leave to simmer for a further 15 minutes. Remove from heat.
6. Serve.

Italian Beef Stew

Serves 4

Ingredients:

1 teaspoon olive oil

600 g (19.5 oz) beef, round, trimmed and cut into 2cm (0.8in) dices

1 onion, diced

2 celery sticks, diced into 2cm (0.8in) cubes

2 carrots, diced into 2cm (0.8in) cubes

1 garlic clove, chopped

240 ml (8 fl oz) dry red wine

2 tomatoes, diced into 2cm (0.8in) cubes

480 ml (16 fl oz) Napolitana sauce

4 red potatoes, diced into 2cm (0.8in) cubes

1 tablespoon basil, dried

2 tablespoons mixed herbs

480 ml (16 fl oz) beef stock

Salt and pepper

Method:

1. Heat the oil in a large pot over a medium high heat. Cook the beef in batches in hot oil until brown. Remove the browned beef to a plate.
2. Add the onion, celery and carrots into the pot, cook for 2–3 minutes then add the garlic.
3. Pour in the red wine, bring to boil then add tomato and Napolitana sauce. Stir.
4. Return the beef to the pot then add the potato, basil, mixed herbs and beef stock. Season.
5. Reduce the heat to a low simmer cook for 2–3 hours stirring occasionally.
6. When the meat is tender and the potatoes are cooked turn off the heat and allow to rest for 10 minutes.
7. Serve.

Roast

Allow 250 g (8.8 oz) meat per person

Ingredients:

Beef/Pork/Lamb/Chicken

Fresh herbs

3 garlic cloves

Oil

Salt and pepper

Method:

1. Preheat the oven to 170°C (325°C).
2. Get your choice of meat or poultry.
3. Season the meat and rub with a little oil.
4. Make some slits into your choice of meat and push the garlic cloves into it.
5. Place your choice of herbs over the meat.
6. Cover the meat with foil and place into your preheated oven.
7. Cook for the required time.*
8. Remove cover and finish cooking.
9. Leave to rest for 10 minutes before cutting.
10. Serve with gravy.

* Note: Cooking times:

Cook covered in foil for ¾ of time then uncover for the remaining time.

	Rare	Medium	Well Done
Pork per kg	NO	NO	1hr+
Beef per kg	30 min	45-50 mins	1hr+
Lamb per kg	35 mins	50 mins	1hr+
Chicken per kg	NO	NO	1hr+

Pizzas and Doughs

Basic Pizza Dough

Makes 3 Pizza Bases

Ingredients:

3 teaspoons dry instant yeast

750 ml (1.25 pints) warm water

6 tablespoons olive oil, plus extra for greasing

60 g (2 oz) wholemeal (whole wheat) flour

2 teaspoons salt

600 g (21 oz) plain flour, plus extra for dusting

Method:

1. Put the yeast in a large bowl, add the warm water and leave for 10 minutes until it dissolves and becomes creamy.
2. Stir the olive oil, wholemeal flour, salt and plain flour into the yeast mixture. Mix well until combined.★
3. Tip the dough out onto a lightly floured surface and knead until smooth and elastic.
4. Lightly rub the dough surface with olive oil and place in a clean bowl. Cover with a damp cloth and set aside in a warm place to double in volume, about 45 minutes.
5. Turn the dough out onto a lightly floured surface and knead again (punch down). Divide into 3 equal rounds and rest for another 3 minutes.
6. Roll out each with a rolling pin, or use your hands formed into a 30cm (12 in) round.

★ Note: Make sure when you're mixing the flour into the yeast mixture that there are no flour pockets (that is flour that didn't mix through).

Mamma's Pizza Dough

Makes 3 Pizza Bases

Ingredients:

50 g (1.7 oz) fresh yeast

430 ml (14 fl oz) warm water

500 g (17.5 oz) strong white bread flour, plus extra for dusting

3 teaspoons salt

3 tablespoons olive oil, plus extra for greasing

Method:

1. In large bowl dissolve the yeast in the warm water. Set aside for 10 minutes until it dissolves and becomes creamy.

2. Sift the flour and salt into a clean bowl and make a well in the center. Pour in the yeast mixture and mix well.

3. Slowly add the olive oil. When the dough comes together, tip it out onto a lightly floured surface and knead until smooth and elastic.

4. Lightly rub the dough ball with oil and return it to the cleaned bowl. Cover with damp cloth and set aside in a warm place until doubled in volume, about 45 minutes.

5. Tip the dough out again onto a lightly floured surface and knead (punch back) lightly. Divide the dough into 3 equal rounds and set aside to rest for another 5 minutes.

6. Roll out each ball on a lightly floured surface, using a rolling pin or your hands, to a 30cm (12in) round.

Gluten-free Pizza Dough

Makes 3 Pizza Bases

Ingredients:

2 teaspoons dry yeast

375 ml (12 fl oz) warm water

425 g (15 oz) gluten-free plain flour, plus extra for dusting

1 teaspoon salt

3 tablespoons olive oil, 1 to rub on the dough so it does not dry out

Method:

1. Pour the yeast into a large bowl, add the warm water and set aside for 10 minutes until the yeast dissolves and becomes creamy.
2. Stir the flour and salt into the yeast mixture and mix well until the dough comes together. Tip the dough out onto a lightly floured surface and knead until smooth and elastic.
3. Lightly rub the dough ball with 1 tablespoon of the oil and return it to the bowl. Cover with a damp cloth and set aside in a warm place until doubled in volume, about 50 minutes.
4. Tip the dough out onto a lightly floured surface again and knead (punch down) lightly. Divide into 3 equal rounds and set aside to rest for another 5 minutes.
5. Roll out each dough ball on a lightly floured surface to a 30cm (12in) round using a rolling pin or your hands.

Food Processor Pizza Dough

Makes 1 Pizza Base

Ingredients:

275 g (10 oz) plain (all-purpose) flour, plus extra for dusting

7 g (0.25 oz) fast-rising active dry yeast

¼ teaspoon salt

250 ml (8 fl oz) very warm water (about 50°C (122°F))

1 teaspoon honey

2 teaspoons olive oil, plus extra for greasing

Method:

1. In the bowl of a food processor fitted with a steel blade, mix the flour, yeast and salt. Combine the water, honey and olive oil in a measuring cup. With the processor running, pour the water mixture through the feed tube in a steady stream, adjusting the amount poured so the flour can absorb it. Turn the processor off when the dough gathers into clumps and before it forms a smooth ball. Do not over process – it should feel sticky. If it is too soft, add more flour, 1 tablespoon at a time, until the dough has a firm consistency.

2. Knead by processing for an additional 45 seconds or knead by hand until the dough is smooth and silky.★ Shape into a ball.

3. Place the dough in an oiled bowl and turn to coat evenly. Cover with plastic wrap and leave to rise in a warm place until doubled in size, 30–40 minutes.

4. Tip the dough out onto a lightly floured surface and knead (punch down) the dough. Cover with the inverted bowl, and set aside to rest for 10 minutes.

5. On a lightly floured surface, roll out the dough to the desired size. Any excess dough can be wrapped in plastic wrap and refrigerated.

★ Note: A food processor fitted with a steel blade can mix pizza dough in seconds. If your food processor is powerful enough to handle heavy yeast doughs without damaging the motor, you can also use it to knead the dough. If necessary, mix the ingredients in the food processor and complete the kneading by hand.

Bocconcini Pizza

Makes 1 Pizza

Ingredients:

1 pizza base

250 ml (8 fl oz) Napolitana sauce (see page 64)★

450 g (16 oz) Bocconcini cheese, sliced

Handful fresh basil leaves, to garnish

Method:

1. Spread the Napolitana sauce evenly over the base and top with sliced bocconcini cheese.
2. Put the pizza straight onto pavers in a preheated wood-fired oven using a paddle.
3. Allow to cook for 10 minutes, rotating occasionally, until the base is golden brown and cheese has melted.
4. Scatter with fresh basil leaves. Cut and serve.

★ Note: Replace Napolitana sauce with thinly sliced tomato, if you like.

Caramelized Onion Pizza

Makes 1 Pizza

Ingredients:

1 pizza base

125 ml (4 fl oz) olive oil, plus extra for drizzling

1.9 kg (4¼ lb) Spanish onions, thinly sliced

6 garlic cloves

5 sprigs fresh thyme, leaves stripped from the stems

1 bay leaf

75 g (2.5 oz) mushrooms, sliced

225 g (8 oz) goat's cheese

Salt and pepper

Method:

1. Put the olive oil, onions, garlic, thyme and bay leaf in a terracotta bowl. Push the bowl into a corner of a preheated wood-fired oven and stir occasionally until the oil has evaporated and the onions are soft. Remove the bay leaf.
2. Cover the pizza base with the onion mix and the sliced mushrooms then drizzle with some more olive oil.
3. Put the pizza straight onto the pavers in the preheated wood-fired oven using the paddle.
4. Allow to cook for 10–15 minutes, rotating occasionally, until the base is golden brown.
5. Crumble with goat's cheese. Cut and serve.★

★ Note: Drizzle with balsamic glaze to give a zingy taste, if you like.

Barbecue Chicken Pizza

Makes 1 Pizza

Ingredients:

1 pizza base

250 ml (8 fl oz) barbecue sauce

150 g (5 oz) cooked chicken breast, diced★

75 g (2.5 oz) red capsicum (bell pepper), diced

75 g (2.5 oz) green capsicum (bell pepper), diced

150 g (5 oz) Spanish onion, diced

450 g (16 oz) mozzarella cheese

Salt and pepper

Method:

1. Spread the barbecue sauce over the pizza base.
2. Scatter the chicken, capsicum and onion on top, then scatter the mozzarella cheese over. season with salt and pepper.
3. Put the pizza straight onto pavers in a preheated wood-fired oven using a paddle.
4. Cook for 10–15 minutes, rotating occasionally, until the base is golden brown and the cheese is melted.
5. Cut and serve.

★ Note: Try smoked chicken, it's just as nice.

Peri Peri Chicken Pizza

Makes 1 Pizza

Ingredients:

1 pizza base

500 g (17.5 oz) chicken breast marinated in peri peri sauce

250 ml (8 fl oz) Napolitana sauce (see page 64)

150 g (5 oz) red onion, diced

450 g (16 oz) mozzarella cheese

Method:

1. Put the marinated chicken in a baking tray and bake in a preheated wood-fired oven for 15 minutes. Remove, allow to cool and slice.

2. Spread the Napolitana sauce evenly over the pizza base then arrange the sliced chicken on top with the onion. Top with mozzarella cheese.

3. Put the pizza straight onto pavers in a preheated wood-fired oven using a paddle.

4. Allow to cook for 10 minutes, rotating occasionally until the base is golden brown and the cheese has melted.

5. Cut and serve.

Meat Lover's Pizza

Makes 1 Pizza

Ingredients:

1 pizza base
250 ml (8 fl oz) barbecue sauce★
175 g (6 oz) ham, diced
115 g (4 oz) pepperoni, sliced
175 g (6 oz) bacon, diced
115 g (4 oz) chorizo, sliced
450 g (16 oz) mozzarella cheese

Method:

1. Spread the barbecue sauce evenly over the pizza base. Arrange the diced ham, sliced pepperoni, diced bacon and sliced chorizo around the pizza, then top with the mozzarella cheese.
2. Put the pizza straight onto the pavers in a preheated wood-fired oven using a paddle.
3. Allow to cook for 10 minutes, rotating occasionally, until the base is golden brown and the cheese has melted.
4. Cut and serve.

★ Note: For an 'inferno' replace the barbecue sauce with spicy chilli sauce and hot chorizo!

Pepperoni Calzoni

Makes 1 Pizza

Ingredients:

1 pizza base

125 ml (4 fl oz) Napolitana sauce (see page 64)

175 g (6 oz) pepperoni, sliced

40 g (1.5 oz) kalamata olives

225 g (8 oz) mozzarella cheese

Method:

1. Spread the Napolitana sauce evenly over half of the base. Arrange the pepperoni and olives on top and cover with mozzarella.
2. Fold over the other half of the dough circle, and crimp around edge with your fingers.
3. Put the pizza straight onto pavers in a preheated wood-fired oven using a paddle.
4. Allow to cook for 10 minutes, rotating occasionally until the base and top are golden brown.
5. Cut and serve.

Bolognese Pizza

Makes 1 Pizza

Ingredients:

1 pizza base
350 g (12 oz) Bolognese sauce (see page 68)
450 g (16 oz) mozzarella cheese

Method:

1. Spread the Bolognese sauce evenly over the pizza base, then top with mozzarella cheese.
2. Put the pizza straight onto pavers in a preheated wood-fired oven using a paddle.
3. Cook for 10 minutes, rotating occasionally, until the base is golden brown and the cheese has melted.
4. Cut and serve.

Garlic Pizza

Makes 1 pizza

Ingredients:

1 pizza base
6 garlic cloves
60 ml (2 fl oz) olive oil
Pinch of salt and pepper
1 handful fresh parsley, chopped, to garnish

Method:

1. Put the garlic, olive oil and salt and pepper in a blender and blend to a pureé. Drizzle the pureé evenly over the pizza base.
2. Put the pizza straight onto the pavers in a preheated wood-fired oven using a paddle.
3. Allow to cook for 10 minutes, rotating occasionally, until the base is golden brown.
4. Sprinkle with chopped parsley. Cut and serve.

Nutella Pizza

Makes 1 Pizza

Ingredients:

1 pizza base
600 g (21 oz) Nutella
100 g (3.5 oz) strawberries, halved
500 g (17.5 oz) mascarpone★

Method:

1.   Put the pizza base straight onto the pavers in a preheated wood-fired oven using a paddle.
2.   Allow to bake for 5 minutes then remove from the oven. Spread Nutella evenly on the top, then return to the oven.
3.   Bake for 5 minutes, rotating occasionally until the base is golden brown.
4.   Arrange the strawberries on top, then serve with a dollop of mascarpone.

★ Note: Replace the mascarpone with ice cream or whipped cream, if you like.

Fig and Goat's Cheese Pizza

Makes 1 Pizza

Ingredients:

12 dried figs, quartered

1 pizza base

125 ml (4 fl oz) olive oil

450 g (16 oz) goat's cheese

Method:

1. Put the figs in a bowl and pour over boiling water to cover. Set aside for 10 minutes while the figs soften.
2. Drizzle olive oil evenly over the pizza base then arrange the fig quarters over the top.
3. Put the pizza straight onto the pavers in a preheated wood-fired oven using a paddle.
4. Allow to cook for 10 minutes, rotating occasionally, until the base is golden brown.
5. Sprinkle with crumbled goat's cheese. Cut and serve.

Desserts

Tiramisu

Serves 4

Ingredients:

2 eggs, separated
60 g (2oz) caster sugar
125 g (4 oz) mascarpone cheese
70 ml (2.7 fl oz) coffee liqueur
100 ml (3.4 fl oz) thickened cream
240 ml (8 fl oz) strong Italian coffee
16 sponge finger biscuits (savoiardi)
Cocoa powder for dusting

Method:

1. In a bowl mix the egg yolks and sugar together until it turns pale and creamy.
2. Then fold in the mascarpone and coffee liqueur.
3. Whip the cream in separate bowl to a firm peak.
4. Fold the cream into the mascarpone mixture.
5. Whip the egg whites until stiff peak forms, fold into the mascarpone mixture. Cover with plastic wrap and refrigerate for 30 minutes.
6. Get a baking dish 6cm (2.4in) deep, 14x14cm (5.5x5.5in) square. Dip half of the biscuits into the coffee and layer on the bottom of the baking dish.
7. Cover the biscuits with half of the mascarpone mixture, repeat with the rest of the biscuits, then finish with the mascarpone mixture. Cover and refrigerate for 4 hours.
8. Dust the top with cocoa powder and serve. Add fresh fruit with it if you like.

Panna Cotta

Serves 4

Ingredients:

300 ml (10 fl oz) thickened cream
300 ml (10 fl oz) cream
5 tablespoons caster sugar
1 teaspoon vanilla extract
100 g (3.5 oz) white chocolate
3 sheets gelatine

Method:

1. Place the creams, sugar and vanilla in a saucepan over a medium heat. Stir until the sugar dissolves, then add the chocolate. Turn off the heat and leave until the chocolate melts.
2. Soak the gelatin in cold water until soft, drain and squeeze out the excess water, then add to the cream mixture and stir until all combined.
3. Strain and set aside to cool slightly before pouring into panna cotta molds.
4. Refrigerate for 4 hours or until set.
5. Dip the molds into warm water very briefly to make the panna cotta easier to get out.
6. Serve with your favorite fresh fruit.

Chocolate Gelato

Serves 8

Ingredients:

720 ml (24 fl oz) milk

170 g (6 oz) caster sugar

2 tablespoons corn flour

170 g (6 oz) cocoa (good quality)★

Method:

1. Whisk 240 ml (8 fl oz) milk with the sugar, corn flour and cocoa.
2. Place the rest of the milk in a saucepan and bring to the boil.
3. Mix the boiled milk with the chocolate mix and stir to combine.
4. Return the mixture to the saucepan and stir on a low heat until it starts to thicken.
5. Pour mixture into a shallow container and put in freezer until the edge starts to freeze.
6. Remove from freezer and beat with electric beater.
7. Pour back into container, and repeat 3 or 4 times.
8. Leave overnight before serving.

★ Note: Get a good quality cocoa to give a good taste!

   You can always double the quantities to make extra because when you eat a little bit, you'll go back for more! Yum!

Lemon Gelato

Serves 8

Ingredients:

8 lemons

200 g (7 oz) white sugar

5 eggs

480 ml (16 fl oz) milk

Method:

1. Before you squeeze the lemons, peel off some of the lemon rind to mix into egg mixture.
2. Squeeze out all the juice from the lemons.
3. Place 240 ml (8 fl oz) of the lemon juice and 100 g (3.5 oz) sugar into a saucepan and heat over a medium heat.
4. Cook and stir for 5 minutes or until it becomes a syrup. Reduce the heat and simmer for 15 minutes until the syrup reduces by half. Pour into a bowl to cool.
5. Put the eggs, 100 g (3.5 oz) sugar and the lemon rind into a mixer, mix until it becomes pale and thickens.
6. Stir in the milk, and then transfer to a saucepan.
7. Cook on a medium heat for 8 minutes or until it becomes thick like custard or coats the back of a spoon. (Don't let it boil or it will separate.)
8. Remove from the heat.
9. Stir the lemon syrup into the custard then pour into a container, cover and refrigerate for 1 hour or until frozen around the edge.
10. Place into a mixing bowl, mix, then place back into the container, freeze again for 30 minutes and repeat 3–4 times.
11. Leave overnight to freeze before serving.

Pancakes

Serves 4

Ingredients:

360 ml (12 fl oz) milk

1 egg

2 teaspoons vanilla extract

400 g (14 oz) self-raising (self-rising) flour

¼ teaspoon bicarbonate soda

65 g (2.3 oz) caster sugar

30 g (1 oz) butter, melted

Method:

1. Combine the milk, egg and vanilla into a bowl. Mix well.
2. In a separate bowl sift the flour and bicarb soda and stir in the sugar.
3. Make a well in the center of the flour, add the milk mixture and mix well until all lumps are gone.★
4. Heat a large frying pan over a medium heat, brush with little of the melted butter.
5. Pour a small amount of the pancake mixture into the hot pan, cook until lightly brown on each side.
6. Serve with maple syrup, Nutella, whipped cream, ice cream, fresh fruit or any of your favorite toppings.

★ Note: If still lumpy you can strain it.

Caramelized Figs with Chocolate Ricotta

Serves 4

Ingredients:

225 g (8 oz) fresh ricotta

60 g (2 oz) dark chocolate, finely chopped

2 tablespoons pistachios, coarsely chopped

2 tablespoons icing sugar (confectioners' sugar)

8 figs, ripe

1½ tablespoons honey

Method:

1. Mix the ricotta, chocolate, pistachios and icing sugar in a bowl.
2. Preheat the grill on high, cut the figs in half and place the cut side up on a baking tray.
3. Drizzle the figs with honey.
4. Grill the figs for 2–3 minutes or until slightly caramelized.
5. Allow 2 figs per serve.
6. Place the ricotta on top and drizzle with little bit more honey.
7. Serve while still a little warm.

Affogato

Serves 4

Ingredients:

4 x 30 ml (1 fl oz) hot espresso coffee shots

60 ml (2 fl oz) Frangelico (hazelnut liqueur)

8 scoops vanilla ice cream

Method:

1. Mix the coffee and liqueur in a jug.
2. Place 2 scoops of ice cream into 4 glasses.
3. Pour the coffee mixture evenly over the ice cream.
4. Serve before the ice cream starts to melt.

Choc Hazelnut Budino

Serves 4

Ingredients:

560 ml (18 fl oz) thickened cream

350 g (11 oz) Nutella

1 teaspoon hot water

2 teaspoons gelatine powder

30 g (1 oz) roasted hazelnuts

60 ml (2 fl oz) whipped cream

Method:

1. Stir the cream and Nutella together in a saucepan over a medium heat for 3–4 minutes or until smooth.
2. Dissolve the gelatine in the hot water.
3. Stir the gelatine into the Nutella mixture.
4. Pour the mixture into 4 cups or serving dishes.
5. Refrigerate for 6 hours or until set.
6. Top with a dollop of whipped cream when set.
7. Serve with roasted hazelnuts sprinkled on top

Chocolate Tiramisu

Serves 4

Ingredients:

180 g (6 oz) cream cheese, soft

60 ml (2 fl oz) espresso coffee, cooled

45 g (1.5 oz) dark chocolate, melted and cooled

30 g (1 oz) icing sugar (confectioners' sugar)

16 sponge finger biscuits (savoiardi)

60 g (2 oz) Milo powder

Method:

1. Place the cream cheese, half of the coffee, the chocolate and icing sugar in a mixing bowl, beat until smooth.
2. Dip 8 biscuits into the remaining coffee, then layer the biscuits on the bottom of a baking dish 6cm (2.4in) deep, and 14x14cm (5.5x5.5in) square.
3. Spoon half of the cream cheese mixture over the biscuits.
4. Repeat with the remaining biscuits by dipping them into coffee, placing them on top of the cream cheese then finish with more cream cheese on top.
5. Finish by sprinkling Milo over the top.
6. Cover and refrigerate overnight.
7. Cut into 4 pieces.
8. Serve with ice-cream.

Italian Biscotti

Makes 24

Ingredients:

340 g (12 oz) wheat flour

225 g (8oz) hazelnuts, ground and toasted

2 teaspoons baking powder

115 g (4 oz) butter, softened

6 tablespoons honey

2 eggs

Method:

1. Preheat the oven to 175°C (350°F).
2. Combine the flour, hazelnuts and baking powder.
3. In large bowl mix the butter and honey until smooth. Beat in one egg in at a time, mixing well after each addition.
4. Gradually blend in the dry ingredients to form a dough.
5. Divide into 2 pieces and roll into logs, 30cm (12in) long and 5cm (2in) wide.
6. Place on a baking tray lined with greaseproof paper, leaving space between each log.
7. Place into the oven for 14–16 minutes or until golden brown.
8. Transfer onto a chopping board, cut into 1.3cm (0.5in) thick diagonal slices.
9. Place onto a baking tray with greaseproof paper. Return to the oven. Bake for a further 10–12 minutes or until dry.
10. Place on cooling rack to cool.
11. Store in a tightly sealed container to keep fresh.

Coffee and Nougat Crème

Serves 8

Ingredients:

3 eggs

35 g (1.3 oz) caster sugar

275 ml (9.3 fl oz) thickened cream

2 teaspoons coffee essence

225 g (7 oz) soft fruit and nut nougat, cut into 1cm (0.4in) pieces

30 g (1 oz) chocolate, grated

30 g (1 oz) mixed nuts, roughly chopped

Method:

1. Place the eggs and sugar into an electric mixer. Beat together for 5 minutes or until thick and creamy.
2. In a clean bowl, beat the cream and coffee essence together until soft peaks form.
3. Fold the cream mixture and nougat chunks into the egg mixture. Mix until combined.
4. Pour the mixture into cocktail cups.
5. Refrigarate overnight.
6. When ready to serve, top with grated chocolate and nuts.
7. Serve with a spoon of whipped cream.

Index

Dedication:

This book is a special dedication to my father Fortunato, who we lost six years ago, and to my Nonna Dominica in Italy and, of course, the best chef in the world, Mumma Maria. If it wasn't for these people I wouldn't have achieved these great heights in my cooking career.

Thank you,
Ti amo sempre

John Pellicano, August 2015

John Pellicano *has been in the kitchen cooking from the age of 13 where he worked at a function centre after school. Starting his apprenticeship as soon as he left school at the age of 16, in his first year as an apprentice, he ran the The Pointer restaurant kitchen two nights a week while the Head Chef had the night off. From then, John knew he could do anything … if his bosses believed in him then he believed in himself. In three decades of cooking, John went through the ranks from commis chef to the Executive Chef position he holds now. He also spent three years teaching future chefs. John is married to his beautiful wife Cassandra, and is father to their handsome son, Alexander. His first book was Wood-fired Pizza Oven (2014).*

First published in 2015 by New Holland Publishers Pty Ltd
London • Sydney • Auckland

Unit 009, The Chandlery, 50 Westminster Bridge Road, London SE1 7QY, UK
1/66 Gibbes Street, Chatswood, NSW 2067, Australia
5/39 Woodside Ave, Northcote, Auckland 0627, New Zealand

www.newhollandpublishers.com

A record of this book is held at the British Library and the National Library of Australia.

ISBN 9781742577050

Managing Director: Fiona Schultz
Publisher: Alan Whiticker
Project Editor: Anna Brett
Photography: Joe Filshie
Stylist: Georgie Dolling
Cover Design: Andrew Quinlan
Internal Design: Peter Guo
Production Director: Olga Dementiev
Printer: Toppan Leefung Printing Ltd

10 9 8 7 6 5 4 3 2 1

Keep up with New Holland Publishers on Facebook
www.facebook.com/NewHollandPublishers